Shaping Truth, Reshaping Justice

Shaping Truth, Reshaping Justice

Sectarian Politics and the Nigerian Truth Commission

Nneoma V. Nwogu

LEXINGTON BOOKS

A division of
ROWMAN & LITTLEFIELD PUBLISHERS, INC.
Lanham • Boulder • New York • Toronto • Plymouth, UK

LEXINGTON BOOKS

A division of Rowman & Littlefield Publishers, Inc.
A wholly owned subsidiary of The Rowman & Littlefield Publishing Group, Inc.
4501 Forbes Boulevard, Suite 200
Lanham, MD 20706

Estover Road
Plymouth PL6 7PY
United Kingdom

British Library Cataloguing in Publication Information Available

Library of Congress Cataloging-in-Publication Data

Nwogu, Nneoma V., 1978– Shaping truth, reshaping justice : Sectarian politics and the Nigerian truth commission / Nneoma V. Nwogu.
p. cm.
Includes bibliographical references and index.
ISBN-13: 978-0-7391-2249-5 (cloth : alk. paper)
ISBN-10: 0-7391-2249-5 (cloth : alk. paper)
1. Nigeria—Politics and government—1993- 2. Truth commissions—Nigeria. 3. Justice. I. Title.
JQ3090.N96 2007
966.905'3—dc22

2007028863

Printed in the United States of America

∞™ The paper used in this publication meets the minimum requirements of American National Standard for Information Sciences—Permanence of Paper for Printed Library Materials, ANSI/NISO Z39.48-1992.

To Cyril Nwogu (late),
my eternal inspiration.

To Jodi Mikalachki,
for making Oxford possible.

Contents

Foreword*

In the late 90s, Truth Commissions (TRCs) caught on with the effervescence of a newly found cure-all drug. From Latin America, Asia to Africa, the concept was presented as the rite of passage, the crucible through which all of us had to pass to berth on the shores of democracy. Naturally, the effectiveness or the claims of post authoritarian regimes were tested on the anvil of TRCs. The mantra seemed to be: *Have TRCs will travel.* We all took much was taken for granted that in a short period of time, the familiarity of the themes or justice, reconciliation made the concept a bit boring and suspect. The TRC in post apartheid South Africa became the reference point for assessing the effectiveness or otherwise of these initiatives.

Today, TRCs have come to mean different things to different people. Often, observers and commentators have tended to focus only on the perpetrators and in most cases, the more dramatic the particular cases, the more attention and publicity they received. Thus, the cases of Winnie Mandela or Steve Biko for example received far more publicity than the cases of lesser mortals in South Africa. In the case of Nigeria, the issues of the military Generals and the Abacha legacy attracted far more attention than other equally serious matters. These tend to give us only an unbalanced view of the process itself.

Not unexpectedly, TRCs soon became an industry, leading to tissues of Seminars, Conferences and the production of a wide array of literature. As with most of these things, the stories gradually began to become tainted and it was difficult to find the focus because in many cases, we were mixing up apples and oranges. There has been very little attempt in the literature to focus on specific cases or systematize how we might think differently about the

* Vicar General, Archdiocese of Kaduna.

sources of these injustices. In many cases, we have tended to confuse causes and effects and assumed that in terms of models, one-size-fits all. So, the issues of what really constitutes Justice, Truth, and the questions as to whether western legal frameworks and assumptions about Justice are capable of resolving the issues that the TRCs were saddled with especially in Africa. Very often, some of the commentators have taken on so much that in the end, we merely end up with a little bit of everything. This is where Nwogu bravely breaks ranks.

Although Nwogu's work focuses on the Nigerian experience, she pays specific attention to the Igbo position and problematises some of the assumptions that we have had relating to Nigeria's civil war and the role of ethnicity and collective memory. She focused on the Petition submitted by the Ohaneze-Ndigbo who claimed to be speaking on behalf of the entire Igbo nation. The Petition itself was very elaborate and covered a range of issues. It was to my mind, the best written Petition. It was written in an elegant style with a splash of the necessary provocative ingredients which resurrected the demons of ethnicity and regionalism whose seeming nod had been mistaken for a slumber. In the process of its presentation, the Petition also drew the attention of other groups within the Nigerian nation. Although Ohaneze made its case against the Federal Government of Nigeria against the backdrop of the civil war, it was natural that it served notice to the North who rose up to defend itself. This is the focus of Nwogu's work. This specificity is significant because it enables her to focus on the issues of power sharing in Nigeria and the need for the nation to take out its head from the sands of self-deception.

The danger in assessing TRCs in Africa lies in the fact that the South African variant has been presented as the reference point. Yet, as it should be clear to all, no other nation in Africa which embarked on this initiative received both the kind of moral and financial goodwill that the South African TRC did. The reasons are many, but given the fact that apartheid had come to represent the collective guilt of the international community, it was understandable that the world saw the TRC as an occasion to placate its conscience.

Having said that, it is clear that the Nigerian TRC could have provided a wonderful opportunity for the nation to make a quantum leap to the future. Sadly, the Federal Government which set up the Commission seemed preoccupied with the politics of survival than seeking to appreciate the problems of its past. This was the major draw back.

Critics of the HRVIC have focused more on the nonappearance of the Generals and the claims that the Federal Government has refused to release the Report of the Commission. In doing this, we confuse two issues. But this is not the place to go into details. Significant as these observations are, they play into the fallacy that has come to characterize analysts of TRCs. More often than not, armchair critics have paid very little attention to the voices of the victims who appeared at these fora. My experience with the HRVIC is that at the level of the victims who came to the Commission, the numbers that went away sad were very insignificant. Most of the people who came believed that merely confronting their tormentors of yesterday was enough justification for the setting up of the TRC. They believed that surviving to tell their stories was far more than they had ever bargained for. In many instances, when we asked victims to address the issues of compensation, it was not uncommon to hear people say something like: *It will be an insult to God for me to talk about compensation. The fact that God saved me and enabled me to tell this story today is more than I could have asked for.*

In fairness, I am of the view that the first victor in TRCs is the TRC itself. For in TRCs, just watching yesterday's hunter become the hunted and vice versa is something that the arm chair commentators take for granted. For us in Nigeria, most of those who came to the Commission scored the Commission very highly. And, in my view, in the end, it is their views that matter really. But on a broader level, I consider the HRVIC as a window, an opportunity for us as a nation to behold the new world and its new possibilities. More than anyone else, the onus should be on scholars to challenge the nation toward the implementation of the findings of these Commissions by way of engagement. Rather than dwelling on technicalities, scholars of TRCs should do more in seeking to make the case that more than anything else, the successes of TRCs are often to be found in the intangibles and metaphors. For, left to those in power, sometimes, *trading places* can affect memories as the victims of yesterday can easily repeat the mistakes of yesterday by repeating the same mistakes. There is enough evidence of this in Nigeria, South Africa, and elsewhere. Nation building is a work in progress not a finished picture.

Nwogu's excellent work is a challenge for Nigerians at home and abroad to seek a proper appreciation of the complex nature of our national histories and see our struggles beyond the tainted windows of the western media. Her work is very accessible, written in tight and brilliant prose. Her insights and intuitive analysis paint broad strokes across the Nigerian landscape. This work lays a solid foundation for further exploration into the exciting and ever shifting vision that constitutes Nigeria. The best is not here yet, but the possibilities are on our doorsteps. Although as our great Chinua Achebe would say, *it is still morning yet on creation day*, however, democracy offers us an irreversible world of possibilities.

MHK: Palm Sunday, April 1, 2007

Acknowledgments

For the all the help I received in the research and writing process, I am particularly grateful to Gavin Williams, for his uncompromising commitment to the development of the ideas expressed in this book. Other advisors and editors whose help were critical include Jocelyn Alexander, Robert Howse, Raufu Mustapha, Eusebius Mckaiser, Omar Khan, Virginia Lezhnev, and David Magezi. They deserve considerable thanks for meticulously editing multiple drafts, asking insightful questions, and making recommendations that helped to clarify my arguments. Sasha Lezhnev, my excellent copy editor, deserves special mention for his support, particularly his suggestions on the book which led to the formulation of a more accessible title for the book. I would also like to thank my publisher, Lexington Books, an imprint of Rowman & Littlefield Publishers, Inc., and my editors, Joseph Parry and Paula Smith-Vanderslice, for all their assistance.

I am also exceedingly thankful to all my interviewees who are listed at the end of the bibliography, most especially to Father Matthew H. Kukah and Mrs. Chinwe Uwandu who put me in contact with members of the Nigerian truth commission, and answered constant calls regarding questions that developed in the writing process.

Special thanks to my good friend, Nene Okunna, for her help in navigating some of the complex situations that I encountered in the field. I am thankful to the Oxford University International Development Center/ Queen Elizabeth House librarians, especially Gill Short, for all their help in locating research materials. Thanks also to the University of Michigan Law School librarians who also helped to locate research materials and ensured that my books were never taken away from my carrel during my time at Michigan.

The Cyril Foster Fund, African Studies Committee Grant, Queen Elizabeth House Travel Fund, and St Antony's College Carr Fund provided me with the financial resources to carry out my fieldwork in Nigeria.

Finally, I am ultimately grateful to God for his continuous blessings and to my family, especially Chumy and Ifeoma, Ihuoma, Dike, Ajuu, and Uncle Sylvester Ugoh for reasons that go so much more beyond their unconditional support in the production of this book.

Although scholarly work is often seen as a lonely exercise, the achievements of this book are a proof that it can be a collective endeavor. Its faults, of course, remain completely mine.

Introduction

The fame of South Africa's Truth and Reconciliation Commission (TRC) has engendered the spread of truth commissions across Africa. These state-backed commissions have been strongly supported and funded by the United Nations and other global institutions. In South Africa, Nigeria, Sierra Leone, and Ghana, the commissions were set up by 'new era' governments to officially expose and deal with past human rights violations and to bring about national reconciliation and integration so as to lay the groundwork for a peaceful and stable future.

This phenomenon has brought about new debates in African scholarship that explore the motivations for truth commissions as well as their legitimacy, functionality, and effectiveness in the African context. Scholars of truth commissions posit the moral advantages of such a juridical approach to resolving outstanding issues of post-conflict societies. Among other points, they speak to the 'cathartic' effect of truth commissions on "traumatized" societies and their success in generating new and less threatening forms of justice needed in the high-pressure period of transition.[1] Yet, many other scholars are more critical of the capacity of truth commissions to deliver 'real' justice, arguing that truth is not synonymous with justice.[2]

Not only are truth commissions, conceptually controversial, they are also controversial in practice.[3] The imbalance between the treatment given to 'co-operating' perpetrators who expressly received amnesty from the South African Truth and Reconciliation Commission and victims who must wait to be compensated remains an ongoing debate.[4] Similarly, some Nigerians have argued that the Oputa Panel, as the Nigerian truth commission is popularly known, exhibited bias against ethnic minority groups in their proceedings.[5] These controversies, both in practice and in theory, are largely couched in contested notions of justice. This theoretical issue is the focus of chapter one, where I explore the notion of practical justice as the ideal justice for a negotiated transition.

This book, theoretically grounded in practical justice, emphasizes a key characteristic of truth commissions which is that truth commissions serve the sort of justice that is not necessarily ideal in a contemporary sense. It is realistic in nature, a response to the particular needs of each transitional society with the goal of reestablishing or creating anew, the needed social relations for a stable future. Goldstone asserts that "in a perfect society all victims of human rights abuses will be entitled to full justice: trial and if guilty, punishment. But [countries that utilized truth commissions] had anything but perfect societies."[6] Chapter one presents prosecution, not as an ideal justice which is sacrificed in search of peace and reconciliation as Goldstone proposes but as part of the spectrum of practical justice that can be utilized upon the failure of more transition-appropriate forms of justice. A truth commission that is more pragmatic than moral project, even if it aspires to be both, is part of that spectrum. This book explores the work of the Nigerian truth commission through such a pragmatic paradigm.

Chapter two details the setting up of a truth commission in Nigeria. Nigeria's truth commission, the Human Rights Violations Investigation Commission (HRVIC) was inaugurated in June 1999 by a presidential order. The Commission was mandated to investigate gross violations of human rights within the periods of January 1, 1966 through May 29, 1999. Unlike the South African case, the mandate did not make provisions of amnesty an incentive for the cooperation of perpetrators in the truth-telling process. It also did not make provisions for the compensation of victims although the Commission interpreted its recommendation powers as the ability to recommend, among other things, compensation to victims. The Commission concluded its work and handed in its report with recommendations to the President Obasanjo on May 28, 2002. Claiming legal and political barriers, the government refrained from publishing the report.

Using the Latin American cases as a metaphor for Nigeria's HRVIC in so far as both contexts dealt with decades of military dictatorships, chapter two explores the legitimacy of a truth commission as the appropriate mechanism for Nigeria to deal with its past. Mendez, while suspicious of the argument that truth commissions are superior to trials in documenting the collective truths of a society, affirms that "victims and society have a right to truth."[7] This is especially in cases like Nigeria's where "extra-judicial executions, torture, disappearances, and prolonged arbitrary detention" are human rights violations that were "committed as part and parcel of a deliberate, massive, systematic pattern."[8]

Although its report is not officially published, Nigeria's HRVIC made an impact on Nigeria's socio-political landscape. Chapter three uses, arguably, the most public and embedded of ethnic conflicts in Nigeria as a case study to examine the ways in which the HRVIC interacted with the Nigerian sociopolitical melee. The interaction of the Ohaneze petition and Arewa response, from the Igbo and Hausa-Fulani ethnic groups respectively, presented a narrative of the 'enduring conflict' between the two groups. This book debunks the prevailing idea that this interaction was an instance of ethnic participation in politics. Rather, the book reveals that it was the politicization of ethnicity by elite members of these ethnic groups who utilized the official and moral forum that truth commissions provide to revitalize ethnic identities for the purpose of elite political and ideological aspirations.

Chapter four highlights the ways in which unintended events can be exacerbated by the absence of a strategy sensitive to the histo-political habits of the country in the creation of a truth commission. While some of these unplanned developments may have positively impacted on the legitimacy of the HRVIC, the same developments may have also compromised its effectiveness. Despite these events, it is undisputed that the Commission did an excellent job within the context in which it operated by providing a forum that drew the larger public into what is now an ongoing debate about how to heal the trauma of the past for the sake of the present and future. The questions revolve, rather, around legitimacy issues surrounding its creation and its effectiveness and import in light of the non-publication of its report.

Chapter five concludes that the HRVIC public hearings, with respect to the Ohaneze-Arewa interaction, became grounded within Nigeria's polity in so far as it served as another platform for the expression of sectarian politics. Ethnopolitical groups appropriated the Commission as a formal space for the (mis)remembering of histories and the rearrangement of politicized memory so as to mobilize constituencies, claim and reclaim political territories, and gain access to social and economic resources at the national level. Such appropriation, while it may seem to run counter to a reconciliation process, is in conformity with the notion of practical justice in the transitional context since such justice can be (and often is) "accompany[ied by] legal remedies of a distributive nature."[9] However, the Nigerian government, by allowing the case against the publication of the HRVIC report to get mired in legal complexities, undermined its own ability to deliver even the form of practical justice that was available to it. This, in turn, severely limited the potential for justice and reconciliation. Looking at the HRVIC from this point of view shows that the Nigerian truth commission, designed to symbolize discontinuity, in reality reflects continuity with the past.

The book's selection of the petition presented by Ohaneze Ndi Igbo and the response by Arewa Consultative Forum as a case study for exploring Nigeria's

HRVIC is largely for two reasons. The first reason is that the HRVIC, like any controversial political institution or project in Nigeria, cannot be looked at outside the context of ethnic politics.[10] The Ohaneze Ndi Igbo presented its petition against the federal government not as a collection of individual cases but as an ethnic case. The Arewa Consultative Forum presented its unsolicited (not being the accused in the Ohaneze petition) response to the Ohaneze petition as an ethnic defense of all accused individuals in the Ohaneze petition who are members of their ethno-regional group. The politicization of ethnic identity in conflict is prominent in this case.

Secondly, these cases brought key interrelated issues of the 1966 coups, the pogroms and the Nigerian civil war to the Commission. Many Nigerian scholars argue that the issue regarding the civil war (often called 'Biafra war' after the declared independence name of the secessionist part of the country) remains unresolved.[11] Minuscule details, such as that of the historic bight of Biafra being renamed the bight of Bonny, occurred in an effort to bury the name.[12] Dr. Sylvester Ugoh, a high-ranking official of the defunct Biafra explains that "Biafra has become emotive. Biafra signifies secession."[13] The mention of the name is so sensitive that some members of a self-proclaimed non violent pressure group named Mass Mobilization for the Actualization of Biafra (MASSOB) which re-declared Biafra in response to the Kaduna riots of 2000 have been summarily executed, and others are often harassed by the government for agitating for the actualization of Biafra or even wearing a T-shirt with a Biafra inscription.[14]

Amadiume speaks of the advantages of truth commissions as an instrument of social justice, one in which the policy of silence and denial can be reversed.[15] The policy of silence and denial in the post Biafran era about the events leading to the Biafran separation is the greatest harm inflicted on Nigerians as a society. This policy buries the truths about the origins of the deprofessionalization of the Nigerian military, leaving Nigerians mystified as to how and by what means a nation of 130 million can be held at gunpoint by a military minority and robbed of rights, dignity, and identity for three decades. It buries the abortion of nationalism and the birth of ethnic hatred in Nigeria. It buries the truths about the beginnings of Nigeria's decay and degeneration into near-irrelevance. As Soyinka states, "history dogs our conscience and collective memory; everyday still reminds us that the factors that led to Biafra neither were ephemeral nor can be held to be permanently exorcised."[16] Therefore, a study of this highly emotive phenomenon as a case before the HRVIC provides a good opportunity for analyzing the state's and its citizens' commitment to a justice and reconciliation process through a truth commission.

There are four key points to note in reading this book. First, this is the first extensive study on the Nigerian truth commission. The only academic materials on the Commission, to date, are the unpublished personal reflections of Justice Chukwudifu Oputa, the chairman of the Commission, and the unpublished reflections prepared by Father Matthew Kukah, the secretary of the Commission, for a lecture he gave to members of the International Development Center of Oxford University.[17] They were both kind enough to provide me with these materials.

Second, this is a highly specific case study. It does not analyze the overall work of the Commission. However, the micro level-approach that is used here highlights nuances that a general study cannot substitute. The study of the Ohaneze petition and the Arewa response illuminates the degree to which the Commission worked within a politicized ethnic context and the dilemmas that arose therefrom. In doing so, this book palpably explores the role and effectiveness of the HRVIC in this instance. Yet, I believe that it is also important to study the Commission from a general point of view, as this will answer questions regarding the motivations for and the legitimacy of the Commission as well as its overall effectiveness. This is because debating the various issues raised by the HRVIC, from different standpoints, is the key to understanding the limitations, achievements, and overall impact of the HRVIC as a truth and reconciliation commission.

Third, the South African Truth and Reconciliation Commission has been used more expansively than other truth commissions as a comparative case for Nigeria. This is because the HRVIC used the TRC as a standard, especially in adopting the TRC's groundbreaking permission of public testimony and live coverage of the process by the media.[18] It is also the standpoint of scholars of truth commissions that the TRC is the "main reference point for new truth commissions."[19] Though the presentation of the TRC in this thesis may seem minimally critical, it only reflects the perceptions of members of HRVIC in their comparison of the Nigerian and South African commissions.[20]

Fourth, at the time of writing, the HRVIC report was not available in the public domain. Between the completion of the manuscript and publication date, a group of trannational civil society organizations released the report on the internet while still calling for the official publication of the report by the Nigerian government. This turn of events does not affect the analyses conducted in this book in any substantive way. Comments on the report vis-à-vis the contents of this book have been noted in a brief Afterword.

Amadiume and An-Na'im pose the general question that drives this study when they ask: "What are the best strategies for achieving post-conflict reconciliation?"[21] This book seeks, in general, to study truth commissions as a conflict resolution strategy in the context of African ethnic politics. It highlights the ways in which this strategy can and does become embroiled in politics and how preceding and distinctive political contexts that are ignored in the setting up of a commission can politicize and thus influence the procedures and outcomes of a truth commission. Of course, short-term results might differ from the long-term effects of truth commissions in Africa. Therefore, only with time can we answer the questions regarding the effectiveness of truth commissions as a deterrent for future human rights violations and ethnic conflict or as the solid foundation for a more integrated and stable political future for post-conflict societies.

NOTES

1. Richard Goldstone, "Foreword," in *Looking Back, Reaching Forward: Reflections on the Truth and Reconciliation Commissions of South Africa*, ed. Charles Villa-Vicencio and Wilhelm Verwoerd (Cape Town: University of Cape Town Press, 2000); Johnny de Lange, "The Historical Contexts, Legal Origins and Philosophical Foundations of the South African Truth and Reconciliation Commission," in *Looking Back, Reaching Forward: Reflections on the Truth and Reconciliation Commissions of South Africa*, ed. Charles Villa-Vicencio and Wilhelm Verwoerd (Cape Town: University of Cape Town Press, 2000); Desmond Mpilo Tutu, *No Future Without Forgiveness*, (New York: Doubleday, 1999).

2. Stephen Landsman, "Accountability for International Crime and Serious Violations of Fundamental Human Rights: Alternative Responses to Serious Human Rights Abuses: Of Prosecution and Truth Commissions," *59 Law and Contemporary Problems* 81 (1996); Wole Soyinka, "Memory, Truth and Healing" in *The Politics of Memory: Truth, Healing and Social Justice*, ed. Ifi Amadiume and Abdullahi An-Na'im (London and New York: Zed Books 2000); Mahmood Mamdani, "Truth according to the TRC," in *The Politics of Memory: Truth, Healing and Social Justice*, ed. Ifi Amadiume and Abdullahi An-Na'im (London and New York: Zed Books 2000).

3. Amy Gutmann and Dennis Thompson, "The Moral Foundations of Truth Commissions," in *Truth V. Justice* , ed. Robert Rotberg and Dennis Thompson (New Jersey: Princeton University Press, 2000); Johnny de Lange, "The Historical Contexts, Legal Origins and Philosophical Foundations of the South African Truth and Reconciliation Commission," in *Looking Back, Reaching Forward: Reflections on the Truth and Reconciliation Commissions of South Africa*, ed. Charles Villa-Vicencio and Wilhelm Verwoerd (Cape Town: University of Cape Town Press, 2000).

4. Patricia Valdez, "The Right to Truth," in *After the TRC: Reflections on Truth and Reconciliation in South Africa*, ed. Wilmot James and Linda Van De Vijver (Cape Town: David Phillips Publishers, 2000); For similar strains of the argument, see also Lyn Graybill and Kimberly Lanegran, "Introduction to Special Issue on TRCs: Truth, Justice, and Reconciliation in Africa: Issues and Cases," *African Studies Quarterly* 8, no.1: (2004) [online]: <http://web.africa.ufl.edu/asq/v8/v8i1a1.htm> (February 28, 2007); James L. Gibson, "Truth, Justice, and Reconciliation: Judging the Fairness of Amnesty in South Africa," *American Journal of Political Science* 46 (2002): 540-556; Elizabeth Stanley, "Evaluating the Truth and Reconciliation Commission," *Journal of*

Modern African Studies 39 (2001):525-546; Nahla Valji, "South Africa: No Justice Without Reparation," Open Democracy, <http://www.opendemocracy.net/debates/article.jsp?id=5&debateId=130&articleId=1326> (January 21, 2007).

5. Chief Dappa-Biriye, Chairman of the South-South People's Conference, interview by author, Port Harcourt, Nigeria, September 11, 2003.

6. Goldstone, "Foreward," ix.

7. Juan E. Mendez, "Latin American Experiences of Accountability," in *The Politics of Memory: Truth, Healing and Social Justice*, ed. Ifi Amadiume and Abdullahi An-Na'im (London and New York: Zed Books 2000), 128.

8. Mendez, "Latin American Experiences," 128.

9. Ruti Teitel, *Transitional Justice* (New York: Oxford University Press, 2000), 218.

10. There is vast literature that explores ethnic (and religious) discourses of Nigerian politics and conflict. To mention a few, see Post and Vickers (1973), Suberu (2001), Ikelegbe (2001), Ukiwo (2003).

11. Wole Soyinka, The Open Sore of a Continent: A Personal Narrative of the Nigerian Crisis (Oxford: Oxford University Press, 1996); Ifi Amadiume, "Biafra and Intellectual Responsibility," in *The Politics of Memory: Truth, Healing and Social Justice*, ed. Ifi Amadiume and Abdullahi An-Na'im (London and New York: Zed Books 2000).

12. Nneoma V. Nwogu, "Ethnic Revivalism: Recasting the Legacy of the Nigerian Civil War" (BA Thesis, Wellesley College, 2002), 5.

13. Nwogu, "Ethnic Revivalism," 5.

14. Nwogu, "Ethnic Revivalism," 5; See also, "Nigeria: The Bakassi Boys: The Legitimization of Torture and Murder," *Human Rights Watch* 14, no. 5(A) (May 2002)[online]: <http://hrw.org/reports/2002/nigeria2/index.htm#TopOfPage> (February 27, 2007).

15. Ifi Amadiume and Abdullahi An-Na'im, "Introduction: Facing Truth, Voicing Justice," in *The Politics of Memory: Truth, Healing and Social Justice*, ed. Ifi Amadiume and Abdullahi An-Na'im (London and New York: Zed Books 2000), 7.

16. Soyinka, *The Open Sore of a Continent*, 32.

17. However, there are a number of editorials and analyses published in newspapers and the websites of many civil society and ethnic organizations.

18. Priscilla B. Hayner, "Same Species, Different Animal: How South Africa Compares to Truth Commissions World-wide," in *Looking Back, Reaching Forward: Reflections on the Truth and Reconciliation Commissions of South Africa*, ed. Charles Villa-Vicencio and Wilhelm Verwoerd (Cape Town: University of Cape Town Press, 2000); Robert Rotberg, "Truth Commissions and the Provision of Truth, Justice, and Reconciliation," in *Truth V. Justice* , ed. Robert Rotberg and Dennis Thompson (New Jersey: Princeton University Press, 2000).

19. Hayner, "Same Species, Different Animal," 33.

20. For literature that address the limitations of the South African TRC, see Stanley (2001), (Gibson 2002).

21. Amadiume and An-Na'im, "Introduction," 1.

Chapter One

Truth Commissions as a Justice Mechanism

INTRODUCTION

From the dawn of South Africa's Truth and Reconciliation Commission (TRC), a key question that prodded the legitimacy of the TRC was the standing of a truth commission as a justice instrument. As Kiss notes, one response proffered by the TRC's Final Report argued that "even if the South African transition had occurred without any amnesty agreement, even if criminal prosecution had been politically feasible, prosecution would have yielded much less truth about what happened."[1] It argued that prosecution was merely a means of justice and a truth commission was yet another form with the latter, being "a more ambitious" form of justice that insinuated its superior status on the justice scale.[2] More recently, President Johnson-Sirleaf of Liberia in launching a truth commission rather than a war crimes court (that was pushed for by segments of the society) as the justice mechanism for dealing with Liberia's conflict-ridden past said, "I believe that when truth is told, humanity is redeemed from the cowardice claws of violence."[3] In effect, she deemed the collection and airing of historical truths as a better way to deal with Liberia's past than a war crimes court. Besides political figures, scholars have argued similar strands of the apologetic arguing that trials could not "adequately engage with those nuances" that plagued the definitions of victims and perpetrators in the long history of repression.[4] Therefore, "a restorative justice approach, focusing on the victims and on reintegration of offenders rather than retributive justice ascribed to the criminal law, was preferable."[5]

On the other hand, a significant number of transitional justice scholars view truth commissions as "a compromise between the morally ideal and the politically possible."[6] The primary assumption underlying this line of reasoning is encapsulated in Goldstone's statement that justice in a perfect society translates into "trial and if guilty, punishment."[7] As such, the form of justice that truth commissions serve is a compromised form of justice that obtains other needed social virtues of peace and reconciliation. It serves the social needs of the society with the resources available to the particular society. In this sense, restorative justice, understood to be the sort of justice that truth commissions deliver stands as the next best thing to prosecution's retributive justice and is preferred for its compatibility with peace and reconciliation.

Rather than align the framework for analyzing the Nigerian HRVIC with either of the two schools of thought on truth commissions, this chapter will take a more teleological approach to transitional justice and then contextualize its finding in the key elements of Nigeria's transitional status. Such a framework not only provides the ideal form of justice for Nigeria's confrontation with its past, but also provides the standard with which the successes and failures of HRVIC is measured vis-à-vis the Ohaneze and Arewa petitions.

WHAT IS JUSTICE?

To ask whether truth is justice, one must ask what justice is. Contemporary scholars do not attempt to define justice in a conclusive way. Rather, any answer to the question starts from the basis of having realized that the question, '*What is Justice?*' is a question of how *we* define justice. In this translation of the question, the 'we' indicates a situatedness in different times and spaces, and these factors influence the answer that is arrived at. The nature of justice, as with most other socio-political virtues, becomes "essentially contestable," as Gallie states that while we agree on the abstract notion of justice, its application in reality "inevitably involves endless disputes about their [*sic*] proper uses."[8]

The answer to the question of justice can be answered prospectively. Justice is the guiding principle that arises out of the creation or renewal (as in transitional circumstances) of any society or partnership that seeks to establish rules within which all participants can relate to each other. Thus, Barry argues that "a theory of justice is a theory about the kinds of social arrangement that can be defended."[9] Early philosophers such as Hume posited this definition of justice arising from the creation of social arrangements. Hume defines justice as a mechanism for preserving social order since it is used to resolve disputes between social beings who make incompatible claims on relatively abundant but limited resources.[10] This perspective of justice is one which, by being forward-looking, contemplates the development of conflict.

The question of justice can also be tackled from a more retroactive perspective, with the question of justice arising in the context where agreed social arrangements have been disturbed by the deviation of one or more participants. For Llewellyn and Howse, "justice is a response to a powerful moral intuition that 'something must be done,' that something (someone) has disturbed the way things ought to be and something must be done to right the wrong, to make things right."[11]

Either way, justice operates in the context of social relations. As Rawls defines justice, it is "the first virtue of social institutions" which precedes all moral values that society may seek to realize and is consequently the prime social value. [12] Thus, justice as applied in any context ought to be about social relations. Even in more individually focused definitions of justice such as the Platonic notion of justice translated by the Justinian Institute as a "set and constant purpose to give every man his due,"[13] whatever is due to each is determined by what is available to all. Therefore, a primary element in the application of justice is the goal of arranging, re-arranging, repairing, or maintaining social relations.

Rawls proposes that the people who come into this social arrangement must be people with equal powers. According to Rawls,

> [T]he acceptance of the principles of justice as a compromise between persons of roughly equal power who would enforce their will on each other if they could, but who, in view of the equality of forces amongst them and for the sake of their peace and security, acknowledge certain forms of conduct insofar as prudence seems to require. Justice is thought of as a pact between rational egoists the stability of which is dependent on a balance of power.[14]

As such, beyond social relations, the proper application of justice ought to apply in situations of equality. Put differently and more strictly, injustice can only occur in spaces of inequality or power imbalance. Furthermore, justice is a means of maintaining balance and not just a social virtue for its own sake. Conceptions of applied justice such as retributive, restorative, or distributive theories of justice must then include these primary elements of justice.

Since general definitions of justice can be quite abstract and not very useful in their application to social realities, Campbell shows that in less abstract conceptions of justice, we find that there are generally positive or negative ways out of which we derive our ideas of justice.[15] Justice as a language of complaint and sometimes revenge is a reflection of a sense of injustice or grievance that commands a powerful emotive force. Campbell contends that such a language, rooted in the consciousness of having been wronged, presents justice as a negative virtue in so far as it is righting wrongs inflicted on people, and thus the imperative lies on how *not* to treat each other.[16] In the instance of injustice the righting of wrongs then "involves punishment, compensation, or some other way of addressing the injustice" that occurred.[17] Justice, therefore, seeks to regain the societal balance. There are also positive conceptions of justice such as the Rawlsian theory of justice as fairness, derived from an original position about how we should treat each other.[18] Such a notion is created out of what constitutes justice, including perceptions of just social relations within a society, and goes beyond the mere righting of wrongs. It is creative and not reactive. It can be, as Campbell argues, "a set of principles for assessing social and political institutions."[19]

Does a transitional society's use of a justice mechanism occur in periods of power balance or imbalance? Is such a mechanism primarily concerned with social relations? Does such a mechanism derive from a negative or positive conception of justice? That is, does the mechanism act to restore or create equality of powers, or does it act to preserve one? Using Campbell's negative/positive categories, the traditional retributive and restorative conceptions of transitional justice fall within the negative language of justice as they are concerned with the righting of wrongs. Since "conceptions of justice represent differing views on the proper content of these principles,"[20] the next section looks at the contents of retributive and restorative concepts of justice as they occur in transitional societies and their underlying principles to gauge the extent to which they contribute to a just society.

TRANSITIONAL SOCIETIES: BALANCING THE PAST WITH THE FUTURE

While most political scientists define transition in terms of a movement towards liberalization, Ruti Teitel defines it in the contemporary period to incorporate a normative component.[21] By this definition, Teitel delineates particular transitional societies. As such, the first element of transitional societies is their movement from repressive to liberal regimes, repressive regimes being understood to encompass the spectrum of unjust democracies to totalitarian military regimes.[22] In this context, South Africa's Botha-led limited "democracy" can be analogized to Nigeria's Abacha-led military rule vis-à-vis their repressive status. The transition of authority from one party to another in a standard democratic system does not fall within the notion of transitional societies. What distinguishes transitional societies from other transitioning societies in the Teitelian normative understanding is the movement from an authoritarian to a democratic regime that *claims a break with the authoritarian predecessor and a moral political mission.* Such a mission primarily aims to right the wrongs of the past and restore a peaceful, stable state that upholds the rights of its citizens. The inception of contemporary transitional societies began with Germany in the aftermath of World War II and has spread through Eastern Europe, Latin America, and Africa.

The moral mission of a transitioning society involves a general recognition by the new government of the need to deal with wrongs of the past, both to distinguish itself from predecessor governments and to resolve the outstanding harms generated by the wrongful acts of the predecessor governments. There have historically been three ways that a transitional government could achieve this aim.[23] First, it can opt to 'forget' the past through a *de facto* amnesty (no-action) or by officially granting a blanket amnesty so as to obstruct individuals from resurrecting the past through judicial processes. An official amnesty is then a prohibition against picking old wounds. Second, it can prosecute a number of the perpetrators of human rights violations. Third, it can establish a truth commission to ascertain as much information as possible about past abuses and through it create ways to ensure that those violations are not repeated; victims are compensated for the wrongs committed against them; and perpetrators are also dealt with in a myriad of manners depending on the nature of the truth commission. A fourth option can utilize any creative combination of the options to address the particular needs of the socio-historical period. While it is the case that a combination can work for particular societies, there is usually a primary mechanism. For example, in South Africa, while there was a need for all three options (amnesty for truth and in its absence, prosecution), the truth commission was the primary mechanism upon which the other two were contingent. We will deal with each one and the type of justice that it presents in its discrete form.

Blanket Amnesty

Amnesty is deemed a legitimate tool for transitional societies to deal with the past. It is seen to have been "highly effective in curbing abuses when implemented in a credible way, even in such hard cases as El Salvador and Mozambique."[24] Similarly, *de facto* amnesty, which is one in which the government takes no action with respect to human rights violations that occurred prior to its coming into power, is also seen to be successful in "ending atrocities when combined with astute political strategies to advance political reforms."[25] This is the case in Namibia. In cases where scratching the itch of the past could possibly undercut progress, Snyder asserts that amnesty can serve as the "necessary first step in the process of consolidating peace, the rule of law and democracy."[26] This, he argues is "especially true of divided societies where prosecutions risk backlash from spoilers but also threaten to further cleavages between groups whose cooperation is critical to future governance."[27]

It is unclear whether amnesty as a justice mechanism involves the two elements of justice identified earlier in the chapter. A transitional government that grants amnesty or does nothing at all (*de facto* amnesty), cannot be said to involve the victims of past violations or society in general, even if it negotiates with perpetrators. It definitively lacks the negative language of justice in so far as neither the space for complaints nor the righting of wrongs is absent. Rather, it is couched more so in the positive language of justice, because although the act may seem to be dealing with the past (or not in the case of *de facto* amnesty), it is motivated solely by what it believes to be the future needs of the society. Thus, it is neither retributive nor restorative. Yet in its positive formulation, it is also not distributive.

It is also unclear whether amnesties occur in spaces of power equilibrium. Would all stakeholders choose amnesty as the option for dealing with the past if they all were equal in power? It is hard to argue that victims and society alike would choose a justice mechanism that demands nothing of perpetrators of human rights violations. It can only encourage a culture of impunity and impunity suggests that the space in which amnesty occurs cannot be one of equality.

Furthermore, the option of blanket amnesty undermines a government's moral claim to being a 'transitional' government since that claim depends on its actions towards bringing justice into a society that has experienced injustice. As such, it is "unacceptable and should be rejected by any decent people who have any feeling for justice or empathy for victims."[28] Empathy for victims and thirst for justice are not the only reasons that make this option unacceptable. It de-legitimizes the moral claim of the transitional government. This is because the option, even if the transitional government distances itself from or condemns past injustice, indicates that justice does not incorporate the righting of past wrongs, or worse that injustice can be carried out with impunity. Additionally, the establishment of a peaceful and stable society is not viable where past conflicts are not resolved since historical evidence has shown that the non-resolution of conflicts engendered by injustices can only breed further conflict.

Prosecution

Prosecution is often seen as the most ideal method of effecting justice in a post conflict situation. Often prosecutions have occurred in post-conflict societies where the transitional government commands a decisive victory over its predecessor. This is the case for Rwanda and Yugoslavia. Despite Mamdani's distinction between prosecution and revenge, where the latter is particularly a victor's justice, prosecution in most transitional societies is often a victor's justice. This victor's justice where perpetrators from past regimes are at the mercy of the new regime was most famously illustrated in the Nuremberg and Tokyo trials. It is the modern day quintessence of retributive justice and serves both as justice in the face of injustice as well as a deterrent against renewed injustice for the new society in the making. As a retributive idea, Llewelleyn and Howse assert that "[prosecution] is concerned with restoration of equality in social relations . . . and it identifies the achievement of social equality with a particular set of historical practices often known as punishment."[29]

Despite the popularity of prosecution, transitional justice scholars have identified many problems with this approach. Criminologists have debunked the instrumentalist argument that prosecution is an effective deterrent against future violations.[30] With the high rates of recidivisim, it has been proven that punishment alone has not succeeded in decreasing crime rates.[31] Retributivists also tend to stress the moral underpinnings of retributive justice: retribution is not grounded in vengeance, but rather in the notion that wrongdoers should receive their 'just deserts.'[32] Such a justification eclipses the idea of justice as arranging or repairing social relations and focuses on the "ethereal evening of scores."[33] This explanation of retributive justice emphasizes the reality that such a justice mechanism must operate in spaces of unequal power to be successful. According to Llewellyn and Howse,

> Retributivist justice recognizes that harm from wrongdoing extends beyond the individual to the relationship between the wrongdoers, those affected by their acts directly, and the community of which they are a part. However, even while it recognizes the relational nature of justice and the aim of restoring social equality, it misses the mark with the way it tries to effect restoration. Wright points to perhaps the clearest example of this failure as retributive justice substitutes the King for Society and thus actually fails to involve the community at all.[34]

As such, traditional applications of prosecution apply in instances where the state has a monopoly on power. Victims and perpetrators alike are subject to the rules and demands of the state. This also means that the arrangement or repair of social relations, while argued to be intrinsic to the retributive justice theory, is far-fetched insofar as victims and perpetrators are actors subject to a script. Mertus posits that "the stuff of law—the elements of the crimes, rules of procedure, the dance of witness, lawyer, judge—can only do so much."[35]

The prosecutorial process is perpetrator-centered. The state is the victim, leaving the real victims out of the loop. The key message is for society to recognize that a member has deviated from the norms or contract of membership and the goal is to punish such a person for that deviation. Most views of punishment deny that an individual can have a right that someone else be punished for a past crime.[36] Punishment is not due to the recognition that victims or their relatives have a right to the punishment of a perpetrator but of deterrence which is "a consequence of a collective goal imposed by the policy of protecting human rights for the future."[37] Therefore, as much as prosecution might serve a form of justice for the whole society, it delivers limited justice to victims.

Practically, due to resource constraints that are often characteristic of transitional societies, it is difficult to prosecute a meaningful number of perpetrators, given the number of human rights violations and number of perpetrators.[38] Some perpetrators stand in for others and for their crimes particularly those in higher positions. In transitional societies where violations might have been committed in huge numbers, the facts surrounding the perpetration of mass violence are more difficult to ascertain when it is in the interest of perpetrators and their lawyers to hide as many incriminating facts as they can. Furthermore, Snyder asserts that prosecution "in the absence of political and institutional preconditions risks weakening norms of justice by revealing their ineffectiveness and hindering necessary political bargaining." [39] Transitional societies with weak justice systems may violate rights themselves if due process is not followed in the prosecution of perpetrators. For transitional societies, economic realities diminish the results of prosecutions, and mysteries surrounding patterns of events are less likely to be solved, leaving the society unable to ensure that such events are not repeated. Most importantly, in transitional societies where the transition is either legally or *de facto* negotiated, it is usually difficult for successor governments to prosecute those who still leverage power over the state, making prosecution an impractical option for transitional governments without the decisive displacement of past regimes.[40]

Prosecutions serve society well by seeking to deter would-be violators, publicly acknowledging the crime that has been committed and seeking redress on behalf of a victim and, more importantly, the society. However, the nature of prosecution hinders its ability to fully address the needs and concerns of victims. Victims' expectations, decisions or perspectives, whether forgiving or vengeful, are subordinate to the laws of society regarding an act of deviation, making prosecution a weak justice mechanism from a victim's perspective. As such, should an alleged perpetrator win the criminal case based on the legal procedures of the courtroom, a victim has no remedy but to accept the pronouncement of the court. Of course, a victim who seeks punishment for a perpetrator would feel that justice is done when a perpetrator is convicted and punished. However, the mending of the relations between perpetrator and victim is not usually achieved through these means.

Truth Commissions

The third option for transitional societies is the establishment of truth commissions, where the motivation is to document the truths regarding past human rights violations so as to mend the broken institutional structures that allowed for such systemic violation of rights and to provide a forum for victims, perpetrators, and society to air their grievances as a step towards repairing the social relationship. The process of reconciliation at the personal, inter-personal, communal, and national level is the visionary aim of a truth commission. As such, in the litigation sense, the case name is not one of state versus perpetrator as in a prosecution, but is more victim versus perpetrator versus society versus state. There is also a perspective that renders truth commissions into a new government versus perpetrator-government process which creates an opportunity for a government, deemed continuous in theory, to self evaluate so as to learn from its mistakes. As such, all stakeholders of the new society are involved in dealing with their past and establishing a social arrangement for the future.

Truth commissions are conceptualized as a means of restorative justice mechanism. Restorative justice is "fundamentally concerned with restoring social relationships, with establishing or re-establishing social equality in relationships—that is relationships in which each person's rights to equal dignity, concern and respect are satisfied."[41] In other to achieve this restoration, any justice mechanism "must be both concerned with the discrete wrong and its relevant context and causes."[42] As such, a truth commission as restorative justice ought to have a,

> Commitment to restoration over retribution, to reintegration over isolation; a commitment to understanding community as an integral part of the creation and solution of social conflict, with an acknowledgement that whether it is focusing on restoring the sufferer of wrongdoing, the wrongdoer, or the community, the focus is much broader than the individual; a commitment to be forward looking, to look at the outcome or implications of a wrong for the future; and a commitment to bring together all those with a stake in the development of that future.[43]

This conceptualization of justice possesses the closest and clearest approximation to the two elements of the abstract notion of justice identified earlier in the chapter. It is fundamentally concerned with social relations at multiple levels, and such an approach either creates equality or preserves a negotiated equality while diffusing its attending tensions if such a mechanism is carried out in a credible way.

Often scholars who are critical of truth commissions allude to the absence of justice in its prosecutorial or retributivist form as though such notions of justice are the most comprehensive of what justice is. As noted by Llewellyn and Howse, "scholars, particularly those from the west, are so attached to the punitive model . . . and are unable to contemplate the success of other models in other times and places,"[44] because the punitive model is customary in most modern day domestic jurisdictions and forms the framework of international legal norms. They cite Herman Bianchi who asserts,

> [a]lthough punitive criminal law is rather a late development in Western history and, in its present form, is a construction of recent modern times, many learned scholars in the field believe in the shaky dogma and assume that our present punitive structure of crime control depends on some kind of external and natural law, having always existed, though in a cruder form, and having survived because it turned out to be more suitable.[45]

However, this is not the case. Llewellyn and Howse quote Howard Zer who states that "community justice has understandings throughout most of our history . . . for most of our history in the West, non judicial, non legal dispute resolution techniques have dominated."[46] Similarly, in many African countries, community justice still exists as parallel structures to the modern legal system. As such, many rural communities as well as social groups in urban areas of African countries address conflict within the group at the community level and often use the modern legal system as the last resort. In this light, publicly-held truth commissions, by not only directly involving active participants such as victims and perpetrators but also the society at large through modern media technology, become a reformulation of community justice within the modern state. As such, the state facilitates the process in a way that allows the justice mechanism to be independent of the state.

Furthermore, truth commissions restore what has been taken away for all stakeholders. For perpetrators, it recalls their humanity without taking away their dignity in the formulaic eye-for-eye format of retributive justice. This is often reinserted as a weakness of truth commissions as restorative justice. The argument goes that truth commissions let perpetrators off easily. This argument is more potent when proposed by victims of the perpetrator, as was the case with the Biko family in South Africa. However, Llewellyn and Howse argue against this notion. They state,

> Just the opposite is true. Punishment in fact requires very little of a wrongdoer. In a retributive justice system the most a perpetrator has to do is to passively endure the punishment. Restorative justice, on the other hand, demands that the wrongdoer actively seek the restoration of the relationship. Punishment can provide justification for rationales wrongdoers use to defend or excuse their actions–justifying for example their feeling of disempowerment and persecution. Restorative justice requires the wrongdoer to face both their victim and themselves with what they have done; it provides no escape from responsibility.[47]

The inability of perpetrators to face their guilt before their community was showcased in the Nigeria case with the refusal of top generals and former heads of state to come before the HRVIC. Such a refusal, while an obstacle to a truth commission process, remains part of the process. For one, as Amadiume and An-Na'im state, "it is the right of society to see that those unwilling to participate in such a project are not part of new governments."[48] Also, the refusal to participate is itself an indictment of the perpetrator, who by so doing publicly vindicates his or her victims and isolates him or herself from the social relationship of the new society.

For victims, the truth commission provides what Soyinka articulates as knowledge and acknowledgement. That society knows and acknowledges that a wrong has been done to a victim is part of the restoration of the process of restoring the victim's dignity which had been taken away by the harm. In the Nigeria case where the Nigerian public is a victim to decades of dictatorship and the attending violation of human and peoples' rights, knowledge and acknowledgment is what a society needs to begin a process of healing. Soyinka states that "some wrongs have a magnitude that transcends feelings of vengeance, even desire for redress in any form." In those instances, he suggests that victims, including victimized societies, may need

> a space of truth that overawes all else and chastens the human, moral dimension. It is not a surrender to evil, not a condoning of wrongs. Perhaps it is akin to a balm that comes after a cataclysm of nature even when clearly of man's making. It overrides grief and despair, diffuses rage, infuses one with a sense of purgation, the aftermath of true tragic apprehension. At such rare moments, memory ceases to be a burden. It becomes a quiescent stock taking, an affirmation of existence in the present and a resolve in defense of unborn generations.[49]

Such a space confronts, recognizes, acknowledges, and denounces what is evil to society as it is done to the victim by the perpetrator. By such a process, a space of truth telling re-establishes the balance of values in the society. Fraser argues that this recognition and acknowledgment is a distinct form of justice beyond redistributive and retributive forms of justice. This form of justice not only recognizes that a wrong has been done, it recognizes the individuality of a victim and aims to heal the abuses perpetrated against him or her.[50]

Also, truth commissions usually mandated to provide recommendations for restoring justice provide a space for victims and perpetrators alike, with their first-hand knowledge of experiencing and meting out harm, to contribute to ways in which such harms can be effectively prevented. Recommendations by truth commission for robust practical institutional protections against violations, also restores a governmental balance. It supports the state is its diachronic self-evaluation and repair by providing the mirror of self-reflection and the means for the state to guard itself against recidivism.

Additionally, in the active step of fostering reconciliation, truth commissions also create a new form of justice that is not a direct response to injustice and is thus generative. The South African truth commission did not aim solely to right the wrongs of Apartheid. It also created a new concept of justice with its appurtenant set of principles to guide the 'new society' that had emerged out of Apartheid South Africa.

In practice, a truth commission has a designated period within which to complete its tasks, and it deals with more cases in less time than prosecutions can manage since it is not mired in the complexities of legal process. Despite the theoretical appeal of truth commissions, the practical manifestations of this option allow much ground for contention. While such practical manifestations differ in each case, the general criticisms of truth commissions are discussed in the next section.

TRUTH COMMISSION AS PRACTICAL JUSTICE

The two expressions of justice in transitional societies have been retributive (prosecutions) and restorative (truth commissions) since amnesty does not address the question of justice and is solely motivated by political considerations. These two approaches change in practice based on who and when justice is being conducted. Retributive justice is a victor's justice where 'justice as dessert' is applied. As stated before, this sort of justice is often inaccessible to transitional societies with negotiated transitions. Restorative justice, on the other hand, is often the way that a transitional government can address the question of justice even when its hands are tried by a legal or *de facto* negotiation. While both retributive and restorative approaches to justice have theoretical and practical demerits, truth commissions allow for a flexible utilization of all three approaches to dealing with the past as needed in a transitional society.

As noted earlier, some form of restorative justice is often the practical first choice in many African cultures including Nigeria. This choice is motivated by the notion of a communal understanding of each individual as part of a collective who derives his or her humanity from that collective. However, the option of retribution is used when restorative justice fails. This approach affirms Michael Walzer's argument that different considerations of justice apply according to what is in question.[51] As such, restorative and retributive justice are not mutually exclusive and may even be complementary. They are suitable for different situations. The compatibility of restorative and retributive kinds of justice is affirmed by Kiss, who argues that the difference between them is more or less one of emphasis and degree rather than kind.[52] As such, their different application in truth commissions falla on a spectrum that responds to the realities of the society in question with the restorative approach as the most practical starting point.

To make good on their moral claim, a transitional government must reckon fully with past wrongs by identifying past violations of human rights, rendering justice for society and for individual victims of past abuses, and reforming the unjust laws and institutions that made those violations possible. To be able to fully identify past abuses, the people involved in those abuses must render their accounts of the events. Therefore, victims and perpetrators alike must tell their stories. To reform unjust laws and institutions or establish just laws and institutions, the truth about legal and institutional processes that engendered or allowed past abuses must be brought to light, so as to avoid the pitfalls of those past laws and institutions. A truth commission's primary goal of ascertaining truth corresponds to these needs of a transitional society.

Truth in truth commissions is ascertained through the testimonies of both perpetrators and victims. In the case of South Africa, testimonies were brought in as "personal or narrative truth" for individuals or "social or dialogue truth" for people telling different sides of a story.[53] In Nigeria, testimonies were marked as claims, and cross-examinations were carried out so as to tease out contradictions within those claims.[54] In both contexts, it would seem that there was recognition of truth as not objective or subjective, but functional. Truths were defined in relation to substantive judicial or quasi-judicial norms. The pursuit of truth, to a lesser or greater degree respectively, was not so much so as to acquire the absolute truth of an unknown event, but rather to form as coherent a picture as can be derived from many perceptions of truth.

Truth is also selectively pursued. For example, the Nigerian truth commission chose to contain certain truths due to the inaccessibility of some sort of palpable justice. For the HRVIC, there was a necessary obligation to suppress truths that could be detrimental to the goal of the Commission. As such, truths were sought and told to the extent that they would not potentially serve as a catalyst for any form of insurgence.[55] Therefore, truth within the context of truth commissions is not an end in itself. Rather, it is valued to the extent that it is a means to address injustice and create a just society.

Kiss states that "truth and justice are intrinsically and not just instrumentally connected."[56] In the retributive and restorative forms of justice that Kiss explores, truth is a means to justice and as such is only instrumental to those forms of justice. In certain cases, Rawlsian theorists argue that "truth is irrelevant or inappropriate to questions of justice."[57] This cannot be the case since even in the retributive form, the court seeks to ascertain truths in order to convict or acquit an alleged perpetrator. It seems that the argument is that truth itself is not justice, as Teitel argues.[58] However, even restorative justice scholars do not argue that truth telling alone in itself is justice. A victim who tells the truth to his family or a perpetrator who confesses to his friend has not done much to further the cause of justice as we defined since justice implicates social relationships that connect the victim to the perpetrator. As such, truth telling must be examined in context. The argument then is that justice in practice requires a number of acts, one of which is truth telling in a social context, whether to a community or to a courtroom. Therefore, truth is a necessary part of justice. It is, again, the practical first step not *to* but *of* justice.

Ruti Teitel propounds the theory that transitional justice "bridges ideal conceptions of the rule of law and the contingent political exigencies of particular cases."[59] Truth commissions make this case most clearly, as they are pragmatic as a choice in the political contexts in which they arise, and yet are deemed a forum for serving the ideal form of justice in that circumstance.[60] Not only does the Nigerian truth commission fall within the parameters of this theory, this chapter furthers the argument that this theory of transitional justice is both of positivist and normative extraction. As such, a truth commission as a vehicle of transitional justice that is practical in nature is and should be apposite in the set of circumstances that call for it.

Many limitations of truth commissions have been identified by scholars based on the experiences of various commissions.[61] These limitations are rooted in its very inception. Practically, truth commissions are opted for in stalemate situations where new era governments are vulnerable to the power of the old regime. These governments are not only transitional governments but also 'negotiated' governments. The commissions aim to ascertain truth with full knowledge and acceptance of truths as partial, thus defying verification. Justice itself, the driving force for truth collection, lacks a clear definition and could not possibly serve as deterrence, and its goal of reconciliation is far fetched since it is not guaranteed that victims feel better about their victimization, real or imagined, nor is there proof that perpetrators feel bad about their actions. Thus, truth commissions are not about justice but exist merely for the purpose of serving the emotional and sentimental needs of society while dealing with the realistic challenges faced by a new state.

Without a purist sense of moral convictions that drives individuals to ideal forms of justice, a state pursues (and ought to pursue) justice primarily with a sense of responsibility. In keeping with Weber's proposal that political leaders should be guided by the ethics of responsibility as opposed to ethics of conviction,[62] this is not merely a maxim but a practical necessity for negotiated transitions which must keep in mind the stability of the society's future. Zalaquett explains that Weber's maxim does not mean that an ethic of conviction implies a lack of responsibility nor does an ethic of responsibility imply a lack of conviction.[63] Rather, there is a "fundamental difference" between acting according to conviction regardless of outcome and acting with a consideration of the "predictable consequences of one's action" in mind. This, he argues, is crucial for transitional societies with high stakes that depend on the negotiated transition.

Therefore, even if a truth commission's form of justice is deemed incoherent in some ways, Rawls argues that we can "acquiesce" to such a theory for lack of a better one. Given the issue of power dynamics in countries which opt for a truth commission, a truth commission is then the vehicle for a flexible justice that is applied for lack of a better one. Rawls states:

> Since we seek an agreed basis of public justification in matters of justice, and since no political agreement on disputed questions can reasonably be achieved, we turn instead to the fundamental intuitive ideas we seem to share through public political culture. From these ideas we try to work out a political conception of justice congruent with our considered convictions.[64]

Thus, a just state cannot execute perfect justice but rather what Rawls terms 'political' justice. It is just in the sense that it executes the best form of justice that is practical, given the situation in which the state finds itself. We will term this sort of justice, practical justice.

Practical justice fits the general characteristics of justice arrived at earlier in the chapter. It is justice, because it operates in the balance of power and is used as a means to reconcile social relations. States utilize it in times of transition and in spaces of power struggle. It is applied in a space where perpetrators and victims, the transitional governments and its predecessors, and society and the government, resort to a compromise given their negative equality, that is, lack of complete victory on either side. It is expressed in both the negative language of righting wrongs and the positive language of setting rules for moving forward. Moreover, it incorporates multiple conceptions of transitional justice, where restorative and retributive justice are complementary and are utilized appropriately to respond to the empirical needs of a transitional society with a negotiated government. Is a Truth Commission the Appropriate Justice Mechanism for the Nigerian Case?

Nigeria's transitional status was derived from the hijacking of the state by military regimes from January 1966, with one interjection of a short-lived democratic regime, to May 1999 when Olusegun Obasanjo became the elected president of the third democratic government in Nigeria's independent history. As such, the Argentine or Chilean historical situations, with their long history of military rule, were in this way more similar to the Nigerian case than South Africa's historical context.

The sudden death of the military dictator Sani Abacha in 1998, who committed atrocious crimes against civilians and isolated the country from the international community, made Nigeria's 1999 transition into a democracy possible. Prior to Abacha's rule, attempts to move from a long history of coups d'état to a democratic regime had been futile and violent. Ethnic tensions and violence that led Nigeria through months of pogroms and a thirty-month civil war from 1967–1970 compounded Nigeria's violent reality. Institutionalized violence, anonymous assassinations, illegal and prolonged imprisonment and detention, summary executions, and other gross human rights violations were characteristics of Nigeria's reality.

The combination of providence in the sudden death of Abacha and the sensibleness of Abacha's Chief of Defense General Abdusallam Abubakar, who took over the reins of government after Abacha's death, actualized Nigeria's democracy. As such, Nigeria's democracy seemed a gift (although there was heightened international and domestic civil society pressure on the military) from a military elite which chose to relinquish some but not all of its power. This elite's unwaning interest in government was immediately indicated in its sponsorship of a retired general, Olusegun Obasanjo, to run for the presidential seat. Thus, though identified as an elected civilian president, President Obasanjo found himself still indebted to those who placed him in power. Even after his election, when the president commanded civilian authority and political legitimacy that could distance him from the military, the power of the military remained a palpable force for him to deal with.

Given the long absence of democracy and the history of the struggle for it, the pressure on the new government to present itself as a truly new phenomenon was strong. Since the new government could not deal with past injustices by exacting a victor's justice, Nigeria's transition can be defined as a *de facto* negotiated transition. Furthermore, Obasanjo could not grant a blanket amnesty nor ignore the human rights violations of the past governments because his military background already made Nigerians suspicious of his government. To distance himself from predecessor governments, he had to deal with the past. As such, Nigeria's situation did call for a truth commission. In choosing a truth commission rather than an international tribunal, Obasanjo hoped perhaps to soothe the hurt of victims and society while taking into consideration the interests of Nigeria's previous but still powerful leaders, so as not to revert the country back into military rule.

Nigeria's commission was largely modeled after the South African TRC. Nelson Mandela, the first post-Apartheid South African president, was propelled into presidency after decades of political imprisonment. On becoming president, he initiated the TRC project. The South African TRC was almost four years in the making with the full participation of civil society organizations, academia, lawmakers, as well as the executive arm of government.[65] Nigeria's democracy, which was unanticipated, propelled Obasanjo into power months after he was freed from political imprisonment. However, the Nigerian HRVIC was set up weeks after the presidential inauguration solely by presidential order. The chairman of the Commission was unaware of the establishment of such a commission until he was called to chair it. Most of the commissioners do not know why they were chosen to carry out this work. Given the acclaim of South Africa's commission, it seemed that Nigeria needed such a commission, but what sort of commission was never thought through before it was established. The mandate was mostly a copy of the South African mandate and a deadline was set for when the commission was to finish its work. The haphazard manner in which Nigeria's commission was set up calls for some analysis of what its aims were, and this issue is explored in chapter four.

CONCLUSION

It is apparent that prosecutions alone would have been simply inadequate in dealing with Nigeria's violent history, since such an approach would have encouraged the already existing policy of silence and denial. Therefore, the use of a truth commission was justified in the case of Nigeria. It remains to be asked whether the HRVIC as was instituted was the appropriate form of truth commission for Nigeria.

The HRVIC largely modeled the South African TRC with notably different elements. In the next chapter, we will explore the extent to which this model played out in the Nigerian context.

NOTES

1. Elizabeth Kiss, "Moral Ambition Within and Beyond Political Constraints: Reflections on Restorative Justice," in *Truth V. Justice*, ed. Robert Rotberg and Dennis Thompson (Princeton, NJ: Princeton University Press, 2000), 69.
2. Kiss, "Moral Ambitions," 69.
3. "Liberia Sets up Truth Commission," *BBC News*, February 21, 2006, International edition.
4. Naomi Roht-Arriaza, "The New Landscape of Transitional Justice," in *Transitional Justice in the Twenty-First Century, Beyond Truth Versus Justice*, ed. Naomi Roht-Arriaza and Javier Mariezcurrena (Cambridge: Cambridge University Press, 2006), 4.

5. Roht-Arriaza, "The New Landscape of Transitional Justice," 4.

6. Lyn S. Graybill, *Truth and Reconciliation in South Africa: Miracle or Model* (Colorado: Lynne Rienner Publishers, 2002), 177.

7. Richard Goldstone, "Foreword," in *Looking Back, Reaching Forward: Reflections on the Truth and Reconciliation Commissions of South Africa*, ed. Charles Villa-Vicencio and Wilhelm Verwoerd (Cape Town: University of Cape Town Press, 2000), ix "in a perfect society all victims of human rights abuses will be entitled to full justice: trial and if guilty, punishment. But those countries had anything but perfect societies. Many of them had fragile infant democratic governments in place . . . some of the new governments were in place only by the grace of the previous military leadership which had the choice, if necessary to protect their own interests, to resume power."

8. Walter B.Gallie, "Essentially Contested Concepts," *Proceedings of the Aristotelian Society* 56, (1955–56), 169.

9. Brian Barry, *Theories of Justice* (Hertfordshire: Harvester and Wheatsheaf, 1989), 3.

10. David Hume, *A Treatise on Human Nature* (Oxford: Oxford University Press, 1739).

11. Jennifer J. Llewellyn and Robert Howse, *Restorative Justice: A Conceptual Framework*, Prepared for the Law Commision of Canada (1999).

12. John Rawls, *Theory of Justice* (Oxford: Oxford University Press, 1971), 3.

13. B. Moyle, trans.3rd, *The Institutes of Justinian* (Oxford: Oxford University Press, 1896), 3.

14. John Rawls, "Justice as Fairness," *Philosophical Review* 67, no. 2 (1958): 174.

15. Tom Campbell, *Justice* (London: Macmillan Press, 1988).

16. Campbell, *Justice*, 1.

17. Campbell, *Justice*, 1.

18. Rawls, *Theory of Justice*.

19. Campbell, *Justice*, 4; see also Rawls, *Theory of Justice*, 10.

20. Campbell, *Justice*, 4; see also Rawls, *Theory of Justice*, 10.

21. Ruti Teitel, *Transitional Justice* (New York: Oxford University Press, 2000), 5

22. See generally, Teitel (2000), Rotberg (2000).

23. Richard Goldstone, "Foreword."

24. Jack Snyder and Leslie Vinjamuri, "Trials and Error, Principles and Pragmatism in Strategies of International Justice," *International Security*, Vol 28, no.3 (Winter 2003/04): 6.

25. Jack Snyder and Leslie Vinjamuri, "Trials and Error," 6.

26. Jack Snyder and Leslie Vinjamuri, "Trials and Error," 18.

27. Jack Snyder and Leslie Vinjamuri, "Trials and Error," 18.

28. Goldstone, "Foreword," ix–x.

29. Llewellyn and Howse, *Restorative Justice*, 30–31.

30. Llewellyn and Howse, *Restorative Justice*, 31.

31. See generally, Snyder (2003); Llewelyn and Howse (1999)

32. Wojciech Sadurski, *Giving Desert its Due: Social Justice and Legal Theory*, (Dordrecht: Reidel, 1985).

33. Llewellyn and Howse, *Restorative Justice*, 32.
34. Llewellyn and Howse, *Restorative Justice*, 33.
35. Julie Mertus, "Truth in a Box: The Limits of Justice through Judicial Mechanisms," in *The Politics of Memory: Truth, Healing and Social Justice*, ed. Ifi Amadiume and Abdullahi An-Na'im (London and New York: Zed Books 2000), 142.
36. Carlos Nino, "The Duty to Punish Past Abuses put into Context: The Case for Argentina," *100 Yale Law Journal 26199* (1991).
37. Nino, "The Duty to Punish," 3.
38. See generally, Kiss (2000), Villa-Vicencio and Verwoerd (2000), Mertus (2000).
39. Jack Snyder and Leslie Vinjamuri, "Trials and Error."
40. Rajeev Bhargava, "The Moral Justifications of Truth Commissions," in *Looking Back, Reaching Forward: Reflections on the Truth and Reconciliation Commissions of South Africa*, ed. Charles Villa-Vicencio and Wilhelm Verwoerd (Cape Town: University of Cape Town Press, 2000).
41. Llewellyn and Howse, *Restorative Justice*, 15.
42. Llewellyn and Howse, *Restorative Justice*, 15.
43. Llewellyn and Howse, *Restorative Justice*, 41.
44. Llewellyn and Howse, *Restorative Justice*.
45. Llewellyn and Howse, *Restorative Justice*, 5.
46. Llewellyn and Howse, *Restorative Justice*, 6.
47. Llewellyn and Howse, *Restorative Justice*, 36.
48. Ifi Amadiume and Abdullahi An-Na'im, "Introduction: Facing Truth, Voicing Justice" in *The Politics of Memory: Truth, Healing and Social Justice*, eds. Ifi Amadiume and Abdullahi An-Na'im (London and New York: Zed Books 2000), 10.
49. Wole Soyinka, "Memory, Truth and Healing" in *The Politics of Memory: Truth, Healing and Social Justice*, ed. Ifi Amadiume and Abdullahi An-Na'im (London and New York: Zed Books, 2000), 35.
50. Nancy Fraser, "From Redistribution to Recognition? Dilemmas of Justice in a 'Postsocialist' Age," in *Feminism and Politics*, ed. Phillips Anne (Oxford: Oxford University Press, *1998),*11–39.
51. Walzer, Michael, *Spheres of Justice*, (Oxford: Martin Robertson, 1983).
52. Kiss, "Moral Ambitions."
53. Kiss, "Moral Ambitions," 74.
54. Interview, Mrs. Uwandu, August 26, 2003.
55. Interview, Justice Oputa, September 12, 2003; Interview, Mrs. Uwandu, August 26, 2003.
56. Kiss, "Moral Ambitions," 74.
57. Stephen Mulhall and Adam Swift, *Liberals & Communitarians* (Oxford: Blackwell Publishers 1992), 214.
58. Teitel, *Transitional Justice*, 89.
59. Teitel, *Transitional Justice*, 213.
60. Rajeev Bhargava, "The Moral Justifications of Truth Commissions," in *Looking Back, Reaching Forward: Reflections on the Truth and Reconciliation Commissions of South Africa*, ed. Charles Villa-Vicencio and Wilhelm Verwoerd (Cape Town: University of Cape Town Press, 2000), 65.

61. See generally, Martin (1999), Soyinka (2000), Mertus (2000), Kiss (2000).

62. Max Weber's *Politics as a Vocation* was published as "Politik als Beruf," *Gesammelte Politische Schriften* (Muenchen, 1921), 396–450. It was originally a speech delivered at Munich University, 1918 and published in 1919 by Duncker & Humblodt, Munich.

63. Jose Zalaquett, "Balancing Ethical Imperatives and Political Constraints: The Dilemma of New Democracies Confronting Past Human Rights Violations," 43 *Hastings Law Journal* 1425 9 (1991-1992), 43.

64. John Rawls, *Political Liberalism* (New York: Columbia University Press, 1993), 150-51.

65. Graybill, *Truth and Reconciliation in South Africa.*

Chapter Two

The Nigerian Truth Commission: The HRVIC

The Human Rights Violations Investigation Commission (HRVIC) was signed into existence on June 7, 1999 and inaugurated on June 14, 1999, two weeks after President Obasanjo was elected and Nigeria's new democracy was established on May 29, 1999. The HRVIC, popularly known in Nigeria as the Oputa Panel, was not established through a deliberative democratic process like the South African TRC, which was enacted by a parliamentary Act. Rather, it was instituted by a special presidential order held to be constitutionally mandated under the Tribunal of Enquiry's Act, CAP 447. The HRVIC was, thus, similar to the Chilean model where President Patricio Aylwin established the National Commission for Truth and Reconciliation without parliamentary participation. Instituted by presidential order, the constitutionality of the HRVIC was controversial, and in the aftermath of the HRVIC's sittings, it remains so. Many Nigerians were initially skeptical of the HRVIC and opined that it may end up as ineffective as other past commissions established under past military regimes by the same procedure.

The HRVIC was made up of eight Nigerians, who were appointed by the President in what seemed to be a random manner. The selection process for the commissioners remains enigmatic to all Nigerians, including the commissioners themselves. They confirm that the private process of selection remained the individual prerogative of the President. As one of the commissioners stated, "the usual practice in Nigeria is that you wake up and hear on television that you have been selected for a panel."[2] The appointment of the commissioners, while seemingly random, was consistent with the appointment of commissioners for such commissions. The reputation of the commissioners were similar to commissioners of other truth commissions in terms of being highly respected members of the society who work in different parts of the public sector.

Looking at the demographic table for the commissioners, it seems that the criteria for the selection of members did take geography and ethnicity into some consideration.[3] However the majority of the commissioners were Christians with one Muslim minority member. Between the first published mandate in June and the redrafted mandate in October, three commissioners were substituted.[4] Commissioners Tura Michika, Daura, and Abayomi were dropped and replaced by Commissioners Bamali, Ngilari, and Odge. The reasons for this change are the subject of speculation. There were no forthcoming explanations for the changes but their replacements did not remarkably change the balance of ethnic representation of the Commission. However, it did reduce the number of Muslim commissioners from two to one.[5]

While the southern representatives largely had positive comments on the composition of the Commission, some northern representatives affiliated with the premier ethno-political group that claims to represent the north were not happy with the President's selection.[6] This disposition is reflected in the criticism of the Commission in an article in a North-leaning newspaper:

> In a fractious federation requiring reconciliation, religious and geo-ethnic sensitivities should have been reflected in selecting the membership of the panel. For the various religious and ethnic divides to repose confidence in the panel, it is necessary for the composition of the panel which was to serve as umpire to reflect the ethnic and religious strength and diversity of Nigeria. Of the seven members only one inconsequential bench warmer, Alhaji Lawal Bamali, was a Muslim. Many major ethnic groups were not represented on the panel. The Hausa-Fulani-Kanuri ethnic groups that have been at the receiving end of the brunt of allegation of marginalising others have only a lone insignificant member who has never uttered one word save during the farewell party of the panel. The composition of the panel therefore, could not elicit confidence from some of the major groups, whose members at one time or another ruled Nigeria and whose tenures were investigated. This was to later lead to series of allegations of bias and hidden agenda from many ethnic groups.[7]

Thus, the question of ethnicity and religion arose at the very inception of the HRVIC. In certain respects, the criticism is well-founded. Given the potency of ethnic tension and politics in Nigeria, the make-up of the HRVIC disregards the salience of the ethno-religious question. It also raises concern when in a country where about half the population is Muslim, an eight member body included only one Muslim representative. Perhaps, the HRVIC's composition was aimed at casting it in an extra-ethno-religious light to distance it from the politics of ethnicity and religion and thus reduce the Commission's vulnerability to politicization. Even such an ideal goal for the Commission was fatally flawed, given the predominance of ethno-religious political discourses in Nigeria and the inevitability of those issues emerging in some of the human rights petitions that would come before the HRVIC. One Muslim commissioner would not have proportionally reflected the Muslim proportion of Nigeria's population and was bound to raise questions on the very discourse that the government may have been aiming to circumvent.

On the other hand, in a country of more than 250 ethnic groups, an eight-member panel cannot statistically accommodate more than one member of an ethnic group. Even a proportional representation in terms of individual ethnic populations will maintain a commission with not more than one person representing an ethnic group. Furthermore, the argument that commissioners should have at least contained members with the same ethnic or socio-cultural identity as the accused is problematic insofar as the selection of commissioners preceded the cases selected for hearing.

Since the president chose the commissioners and the commissioners chose the cases, there are two ways of interpreting this particular issue with the president's selection. It is possible that the president selected the commissioners with the knowledge that there would be a preponderance of cases against people of the northern region. If so, even if there was a fair process of selecting which petitions would be heard, the prevalence of cases against past dictators who were predominantly of northern origin was already predetermined by the historical realties of Nigeria. This scenario, which captures the sentiments of some northern citizens is plausible, if not completely tenable, given that Nigeria's human rights violations have occurred mostly under military regimes led by northern Nigerians.

It could also be argued that even though the nomination of the commissioners was unbiased, the case selection might have reflected the preferences of the commissioners given their identities. This second scenario presents a highly ethnic-conscious Commission. This is unlikely since the Commission went above and beyond their mandate to involve the Nigerian people in the truth commission's process. The head of the legal counsel for the Commission firmly asserted that cases were selected primarily on the basis of what were deemed gross violations of human rights. She states that "The Chairman [of the Commission] was very careful and made extra effort to acknowledge the ethnic sensitivity of the public."[8]

STRUCTURE AND PROCESS

With some amendments to the *Instrument Constituting a Judicial Commission of Inquiry for the Investigation of Human Rights Violations*, the Commission's, "terms of reference" read as follows:

The Judicial Commission shall-

(a) ascertain or establish the causes, nature and extent of all gross violations of human rights committed in Nigeria between the 15th day of January, 1966 and the 28th day of May, 1999;

(b) identify the person or persons, authorities, institutions, or organizations which may be held accountable for such gross violations of human rights and determine the motives for the violations or abuses, the victims and circumstances thereof and the effect on such victims and the society generally of the atrocities;
(c) determine whether such abuses of violations were the product of deliberate state policy or the policy of any of its organs or institutions or whether they arose from abuses by state officials of their office or whether they were acts of any political organizations, liberation movements or other groups or individuals;
(d) recommend measures which may be taken, whether judicial, administrative, legislative or institutional to redress the injustices of the past and prevent or forestall future violations or abuses of human rights;
(e) make any other recommendations which are, in the opinion of the Judicial Commission, in the public interest and are necessitated by the evidence;
(f) receive any legitimate financial or other assistance from whatever source which may aid and facilitate the realization of its objectives.

Besides the change in commissioners, the terms of reference, dated October 4, 1999, contained changes with respect to the period the mandate was suppose to cover, references to particular types of human rights violations to investigate, allowances for funding sources other than the government, and for the extension of the permitted sitting period from three months to a year.[9]

Foremost, the Commission had been initially assigned to investigate violations that occurred from January 1, 1984 to May 28, 1999. This period covered violations from the end of Nigeria's Second Republic through the date when Nigeria moved into its new democracy and Third Republic. The assignment of this particular period generated a lot of public criticism in the press. Since the Second Republic is directly preceded by President Obasanjo's period in power as a military head of state, the public saw the time limit as the President's attempt to circumvent his own period of undemocratic rule. Others made more specific interpretations of the politics behind the period specified, arguing that President Obasanjo was using the Commission as a quasi-legitimate mechanism to carry out a vendetta against the Sani Abacha regime that had imprisoned him. The combination of public condemnation and the persuasive arguments presented to President Obasanjo by the chairman of the Commission, Justice Oputa, led to the expansion of the period to cover January 15, 1966 to May 28, 1999.[10]

January 15, 1966 was chosen as a cut off date not only because it marked the first destruction of Nigeria's democratic status, but also because it pointed to the relevance of coups in the subsequent history of Nigeria. Since the first coup of January 15, 1966, Nigeria witnessed "six military coups and five attempted ones" resulting in an average of one coup or attempted coup per three years.[11] Coups in Nigeria not only situated gross violations of human rights, they also inspired the culture of widespread political assassinations in Nigeria.

All other amendments to the terms of reference seem to have stemmed from the lessons learned by the commissioners after their initial attempt to make a start with their work. With three months to accomplish its mandate, the HRVIC set about publicizing itself to the citizenry by requesting petitions through the media. Without an amnesty clause, the publications were really aimed at 'victims or perceived victims' of 'gross violations of human rights,' since there was no incentive with which to encourage perpetrators to come before the HRVIC. The Commission could summon accused individuals but did not have any legal powers to subpoena them. In this circumstance, the participation of the perpetrators had to be voluntary when summoned. This approach seems consistent with restorative justice, which need not force the participation of a perpetrator while requiring his or her active involvement in the reconciliation process as noted in chapter one. In fact, the cases in which the HRVIC was able to involve willing victims and accused proved to be it highest success. The flexibility that allowed for either possibility, that is, participants willingly participating or shunning the process as a whole, proved Nigeria's HRVIC to be more quintessentially practical since it made choices and responded to events as the cases arose.

Though the HRVIC received over 10,000 petitions, there were many petitions that did not meet the specifications outlined. The Commission went through the petitions to sort out the relevant ones, that is, those that referred to events that occurred in the mandated period and which were considered 'gross violations' by the Commission under the advice of its team of counsel. 'Gross violations' were defined according to the South African definition to include "acts of killing, abduction, torture, and severe ill treatment."[12] Without enough resources, the HRVIC decided to hear the "200 most grievous petitions with the widest implications for Nigeria."[13]

The Commission held a retreat with members of the South African, Chilean, and Guatemalan truth commissions, from which they sought to get some insights into the nature of the work they were to carry out. They also went to South Africa, at the invitation of the TRC, where they had more extensive discussions that influenced "the HRVIC in fashioning and fine-tuning its strategies for the Public Hearings."[14] After its visit to South Africa, the Commission held a one-week consultation with various bodies, which included human rights organizations, academic groups, private sector groups, media groups, diplomatic missions, and donor agencies. Papers discussed in the forum included "Historical Overview of Human Rights Violations in Nigeria; Safeguarding Human Rights in Nigeria; The Response of Business to Human Rights Violations; Media and Human Rights Abuses; and Security Agencies and Human Rights Violations: A Historical Perspective."[15] The aim of the consultation was to

> enable the commission, through dialogue and discussions with organized groups, to have a good idea of what these groups, and so the public at large, thinks and expects of the commission and its work. These groups, in a way, served as sounding boards for the commission, which felt the need and the necessity to gauge the mood of the public as regards its work, assess its feelings, and know from these assessments what will be acceptable or unacceptable to the public. And, of course, the commission also hoped, in the course of these interactions, to keep its work and activities in the public domain.[16]

The commissioners thus conducted the participatory process of establishing the truth commission after they were commissioned. It was during this process that the chairman of the Commission convinced the president of their inability to accomplish their work within the limitations that were contained in the initial terms of reference. This process also helped the Commission to establish credibility with the public and to achieve social legitimacy.

The HRVIC, unlike the South African TRC, was established without an amnesty clause. In fact, provision (d) of the mandate allows for the HRVIC to "identify" perpetrators and recommend "judicial" measures to "redress the injustices of the past."[17] This provision made it possible for the Commission to recommend prosecution of proven perpetrators should they deem prosecution to be appropriate and thus imbued the HRVIC with the element of practical justice that allowed it to utilize restorative and leave room for the possibility of retributive justice.

The absence of amnesty as an incentive that the HRVIC could use to bring perpetrators into the truth-telling space did create some obstacles for the Commission. According to the chairman of the Commission, this absence presented the commissioners with a "headache in terms of evidence." He asserts that without the amnesty clause, establishing truth meant "looking at the warring truths from a judicial perspective and within a judicial process, that is, looking at the evidence presented for those truths; considering what sides to believe by looking at factors such as the impression of witnesses; and assessing the presentations by looking for a balance/imbalance on the scales of justice."[18] He adds that he tried to convince the president of the need for a contingent amnesty clause similar to South Africa's but was unsuccessful.[19] Thus, truth finding for the HRVIC aimed largely to locate truths of statements largely from victims while sieving out unsubstantiated perceptions as best as it could. Though the HRVIC opened the forum for airing all perceptions of history, it seemed to have created some standard of proof with which to identify what would be the collective truth for historical and recommendation purposes.

Charged with the duty to submit interim reports, the Commission answered directly to the president by means of occasional visits from the chairman to the Presidency. The Commission also procured a team of lawyers who served as its legal counsel and provided lawyers for petitioners who could not afford to pay for their own representation. Primarily, the legal counsel wrote briefs for each petition, summarizing it into five sections of (a) names of accused and accuser, (b) main grievances, (c) evidence for case, (d) petitioner's prayers, and (e) possible relief for the commission to consider. All the petitions were categorized under assassinations/ attempted assassinations, murder, mysterious disappearances, assault/ torture, illegal detention, or press gag. The sittings were held in five main cities, namely Abuja, Lagos, Kano, Enugu, and Port Harcourt, so as to increase the Commission's accessibility to ordinary citizens. Additionally, the sittings were aired live on national television to increase the participation of general public in the process and increase the transparency of the Commission that was in search of legitimacy in the midst of much skepticism discussed later in the chapter. This commitment to societal participation, which began with the open forums with civil society organizations, supported the work of the HRVIC as a restorative justice measure, and the transparency motivation in search of legitimacy justifies its status as a practical justice mechanism.

The HRVIC interpreted the terms of reference as a mandate to "break the misery of conflict . . . as well as the misery of silence so that history will not repeat itself."[20] The aim was to know "what happened" and the Commission was to deal with all the human rights violations that followed the dawn of military rule in Nigeria. About a decade short of South Africa's apartheid regime, the Commission was to investigate events in a period of thirty-three and a half years. Within that period, Nigeria had experienced two pogroms, a notorious civil war, seven military regimes, three bloody attempted coups d'état, two 'phantom' coups, one chaotic annulment of a popular presidential election, hundreds of civilian assassinations, hundreds of high casualty ethnic insurgencies, and countless mysterious kidnappings, torture, and killings.[21] The HRVIC was to deal with the violations that occurred within Nigeria's entire independent history with the exception of the first five years, 1960–1966.

THE CONTROVERSIAL PETITIONS

Despite the resolution or attempted resolution of the mandated period for the Commission, the HRVIC still encountered two main controversies that further rocked its credibility. The first dispute pertained to the case brought against three past military heads of state, General Babangida, General Buhari, and General Abubakar, and three high ranking military functionaries, Lt. General Danjuma, Lt. Colonel Togun, and Colonel Akilu.[22] These former officials refused to honor the Commission's summons to testify and account for incidents that occurred under their leadership or alleged directives. As noted earlier, those who declined the summons of the Commission could not be forced to appear before it, because the Commission was not endowed with judicial powers to compel them to do so.

Nigerians interpreted their disregard for the Commission as a manifestation of the internal tensions within a politicized military—the President, a former high-ranking military official and past military leader, was at war with the other past military leaders. These past leaders came across as not just shunning the Nigerian attempt to reevaluate its history, restructure its foundations, and reconcile its society, but as "above the law and beyond punishment."[23] This is perhaps one of the weakest aspects of restorative justice, that is, the unwillingness of perpetrators to participate in a measure that values reintegration over isolation, as noted in chapter one. In the Nigerian context, such a circumstance barring subsequent retributive measures would then affirm the historical culture of military impunity. On the other hand, the generals' refusal to participate was seen as a conviction in itself and provided the society with their "right to see that those unwilling to participate are not part"[24] of the new government. This, as discussed in chapter one, remains part of a truth commission like Nigeria's. Given that the mandate allows for the HRVIC to recommend judicial redress and none of these generals are protected by amnesty, the Commission as a practical justice mechanism should be able to recommend prosecution of the generals since by their non-participation, they have chosen isolation instead of reintegration.

The second dispute was brought to the fore through the petition of the Ohaneze Ndi Igbo, petition 1648, which was presented on behalf of the Igbos of south-eastern Nigeria. This petition generated responses and counter-petitions by other ethno- and geo-political organizations, who either felt slighted by petition 1648 or were inspired to present their own cases. The main responses were the Arewa Consultative Forum representing the north, the Joint Action Committee representing the central northern region (known as the Middle Belt), the Afenifere representing the south-west region, and the South-South Peoples representing the South-South region of Nigeria. Ohaneze's request for an eight trillion Naira compensation, for all the human rights violations perpetrated against the Igbos and documented in their petition, also triggered a deluge of individual petitions that were motivated by the potential for monetary compensation. The next chapter examines Petition 1648 in greater detail.

In sum, these two issues became linked to the extent that these ethno-political organizations saw as part of their responsibility the need to defend accused members of the military who shared their ethnic identity. This was consistent with the public perception of the military as linked to the politicization of ethnicity in Nigeria. As a Nigerian professor writing on the Commission and the military stated:

> It should have been obvious to all Nigerians from the revelations at the Commission that Nigeria does not have a national army, but that what Nigeria has in the name of Nigeria is a *geo-ethno-military* organization. It is an army in the name of Nigeria but operating with a regional agenda.[25]

As the politics of spoils unfolded through the manipulation and mobilization of ethnic religious and geographic identities, the politicized military was consequently entangled in the tensions and rivalries. Thus, the support or denunciation of the actions of ethnic organizations and the military at the commission often ran along ethnic lines.

The Commission dealt with cases related to ethnic organizations and the military with much sensitivity. The ethnic organizations were given the opportunity to air their grievances, which were largely against the state or other dominant ethnic groups. The Commission requested further inquiries into these petitions by assigning researchers and research institutes to investigate and collate the violations against each regional or ethnic group since 1966. Without the ability to deal further with the absence of the controversial military officials, the commission's resolution of the issue lies in its report.

THE CHALLENGES OF THE COMMISSION

Even though the HRVIC was presented as a part of the bridge-building process in a new democratic but severely fractured country, some Nigerians saw it as a southern conspiracy against the northerners.[26] This perception of the Commission was sustained even after the public hearings were completed. As much as some sections of the public politicized the cases that were handled, the commissioners felt that their conduct was beyond the realm of political partisanship.[27] However, the identities of the commissioners cannot be said to have been shed outside of their sittings. The lead counsel asserted that the sensitivity with which the Ohaneze case was handled, so as to avoid accusations of nepotism, was palpable, given the Chairman's affiliation with the people that Ohaneze represented.[28] As citizens who had been embroiled in the daily manifestations of ethnic rivalry and politics for decades, whatever actions the commissioners took were bound to be contextualized by the partisan interpretations that would be given them by the public. It was therefore a realistic possibility that, whatever the disposition of the commissioners themselves, the HRVIC could solidify some of the existing divisions in the country. This challenge once again raises the question of whether the government should have taken cognizance of the high ethnic consciousness of Nigerians in structuring the HRVIC. Perhaps, a truth commission that included well-respected non-Nigerian Africans may have eased the particular tensions and worked better for the Nigerian context.

Second, the military problem was not only controversial in the shunning of the Commission by former military leaders. For Nigerians, the very source of the HRVIC seemed antithetical to its goals of reconciling the past, because it was set up by a former military leader who was still, either negatively or positively, engaged with different cliques of Nigeria's corrupt and ethnicized military elite. As such, the label of a "new era" government was taken to task. For example, Father Kukah stated:

> Military rule was worse than apartheid. That may sound controversial, but it was worse than apartheid and I can tell you the reason. Apartheid with its wickedness managed to leave a sound economy. With its viciousness, it managed to leave a sound judiciary. With all its wickedness, it left a system in place. The tragedy is that, the military in Nigeria destroyed every facet of national life. Unless we understand the level of devastation that was wrecked by the military, including Obasanjo who was part of the package, unless we isolate all that, we can never begin to appreciate the enormity of the problems that face Nigeria.[29]

Seeing Nigeria in these terms, the HRVIC seems to have been set up by a member of the old era, no matter the disguise. It would be analogous to a scenario in which former South African President de Klerk enfranchised all South Africans and was propelled to a democratic leadership with the funding of the National Party or a white minority who had supported the Apartheid system. A South African TRC established under these conditions would have proved less than credible. This problem was one that alienated members of the Nigerian public and led citizens to a more cautious and less trusting perspective of the HRVIC's work.

Third, President Obasanjo appeared before the HRVIC both as a victim of General Abacha's regime which had imprisoned him and as a perpetrator under his own military regime of 1976–1979. Given that he was the source of the HRVIC and was expected to ultimately implement its recommendations, there are doubts as to how the Commission dealt with cases that were related to President Obasanjo's government. President Obasanjo's Chief of Army Staff, though one of 'the generals' that eschewed the summons of the Commission, attended its events as a government official. This duality in the government's treatment of the HRVIC placed the Commission in a perplexing position.

Fourth, despite the public speculations regarding the HRVIC, it was very popular. With live televising of the public hearings, the Nigerian public was very involved with the process. Yet both the Commissioners and the public were convinced that the popularity of the Commission, which was evidenced in the number of petitions, stemmed from suspect motives. As previously stated, the potential for compensation increasingly became an incentive for people to bring their cases forward. Perhaps this was the product of the deprivation that was wrecked on the Nigerian populace by dictatorships that had robbed Nigeria of its resources, leaving most of its population in abject poverty. Nigerians were seeking some form of redistributive justice. Yet, it may be the case that the rush for compensation was indeed another vulgar attempt at habitual spoils politics. Either way, the recommendations of the HRVIC are compelled to prioritize some forms of distributive measure over other measures even if to rehabilitate the country from resorting to the politics of spoils which is engendered by the contested distribution of Nigeria's resources.

Scarcity of resources was a practical dilemma that the HRVIC faced. Those who set up the Commission "did not know the magnitude of the work involved but were truly interested in its effect."[30] The government, while seeking the dividends of a truth commission, did not have the patience to allow for the time needed to create the appropriate and context-specific procedures, nor did they budget the necessary funds needed to accomplish a thorough job. For example, the Commission was given two lawyers when it requested twenty-four.[31] This affected the possibilities for further enquiry and also unwittingly shortened the time to compile more information needed for making recommendations.[32] The Ford Foundation heavily subsidized the Commission's task and helped to fund the writing of the report with additional assistance from the British Council.[33] This particular issue buttresses the argument that while Obasanjo wanted to legitimate the status of his government as a transitional one, he was not particularly in favor of undertaking the challenges of a transitional government. Therefore, he used the HRVIC as a means to distance himself from his predecessors but was not vested in acting on the moral claim that a transitional government pronounces against the past.

The lack of parliamentary involvement, the omnipresent nature of military and ethnic politics, and the possibility of dealing with petitioners with ambiguous motives, challenged the HRVIC's attempt to sieve out human rights violations intricately mired in these obstacles. For the chairman of the Commission, the work of the HRVIC often seemed insurmountable.[34] However, with international assistance, the HRVIC was able to do a job that commanded the acclaim of a large section of civil society. It presented the voluminous report which Father Kukah states was the best work that the HRVIC could do within the context of the pressures that it faced. Thus, Father Kukah asserts:

> We did a job, and I am sure we did that job to the best of our ability. We became the victims of our success. Perhaps, part of the problem and the fear of the government was that the Commission went beyond the lines and parameters that set up the Commission. For now, I will never know why the government has decided not to release the report; but I do not believe the argument that it is about law. I am not convinced about their argument that it has to do with a case in court. The Commission was not under any pressure from any quarters. There were no subterranean meanderings by anyone.[35]

Whether the commission did a good job or not is generally deemed to rely heavily on the report. Pessimistic Nigerians are convinced that the document will be buried in the manner of its forebears in the tomb of disappearance and silence that is part of Nigeria's political history. For less cynical Nigerians, whether the report is published or not, the petitions remain a documentation of history for the posterity of those who submitted petitions and will be the beginning of the change that the country needs.

THE REPORT

The Commission's public sittings ended on October 18, 2001 and it handed in its report at a ceremony on May 28, 2002. The report comprised seven volumes, which included summaries of the petitions and the recommendations for each of the petitions.[36] The guiding rubric for its recommendations was based "solely on the mandate 'to reconcile' and the theme of the report lay in answering the question 'How do we create one Nigeria?'"[37] As Mrs. Uwandu asserts:

> The Commission avoided adopting a judgmental position in all cases, recognizing there are different sides to every story. Their goal was to heal. They did not and could not judge people innocent or guilty. They did not have that luxury. But they could not also believe all the witnesses who in some cases were obviously contradicting each other. The commissioners weighed all the issues and then based their recommendations on the goal to heal the rift between the quarreling parties.[38]

Without access to the reports, the above statement seems to suggest that the HRVIC may have opted not to "name names" of proven perpetrators in like manner to the Chilean case.[39] However, that it may also not have named the names of victims would be unlike the Chilean model. It is difficult to understand how the HRVIC can "not judge people innocent or guilty" and yet be able to "recognize" and "acknowledge" the victimization of those who were victimized. Ultimately, the HRVIC saw their primary goal as establishing the conditions for reconciliation at the individual, ethnic, and national levels, to establish the foundations for a united country. This is also analogous to the Chilean model in which Chilean commission saw its mandate as demanding a document "that takes national cohesion as its starting premise and posits violence as resulting from the dissolution of that unity."[40]

The Nigerian commission also regarded monetary compensation as an aspect of justice in its report and recommendations.[41] They saw reparation as a key requirement for a fragile transitional justice like Nigeria's. However, the president was not of that opinion, and "He argued that the country should not and cannot equate suffering with money."[42] Whether the president's perception had any influence on the Commission's recommendations for reparative or distributive measures is unknown. The extent to which the Commission's view is reflected in the still to be published White Paper, the government's official decision on and account of the recommendations to be implemented, also remains unknown.

The Commission's chairman considered the recommendations controversial even before they were handed in. He states:

> The Commission recognized the contestability of justice in application. Real justice is seen as something that requires peace and harmony, as peace is a necessary condition for justice and this is not assured with vengeful justice. Therefore, forgiveness and reconciliation is the alternative option to revenge or retributive justice. The issue is that despite what choices are made "the pains of justice might still traumatize our country."[43]

It is indeed the case that disagreements would be expected since it is impossible to find a unanimous solution to many of Nigeria's problems. There are bound to be vested interests in the *status quo*, as well as a counterpoint to any perspective the Commission chooses to take. To what extent those concerns will materialize remains dependent on the official publication of the report.

After the report was handed in, the president established an implementation committee under the leadership of one of the commissioners, Mrs. Elizabeth Pam. According to Mrs. Uwandu, this committee was charged with reading the seven-volume report and reducing it to readable form for the executive council of Obasanjo's government. They were to achieve this by accepting, rejecting, and modifying the recommendations. Mrs. Uwandu states:

> The Implementation Committee was unique, because it was the first of its kind in the history of Nigeria. Given that they had no precedence to borrow from,

> they liaised with the legal counsel of the Commission so as to get some help in ensuring the legality of the recommendations that would be presented to the executive council. They finished their work, and the White Paper is now in existence in addition to the report. It was sent to the executive council who actually considered it but before any further action could be taken, the Babangida case obtained the injunction not to publish the report nor do anything with it.[44]

As the above statement indicated, General Babangida, Nigeria's former dictator, challenged the constitutionality of the HRVIC after the Commission had completed its project. He obtained a legal injunction that prohibited the publication or use of the Commission's report. Therefore, though the White Paper and the report are both available, they have not been officially released into the public domain.[45] In December 2004, eighteen months after the report was presented to the government, the Nigerian Supreme Court ruled that the power to establish tribunals of enquiry was a residual power and thus resided with the states, except with respect to the federal territory where such power belongs to the national assembly.[46] Despite this pronouncement, there has been widespread public pressure on the government by civil society organizations, ethno- and geo-political organization, and human rights groups to officially release the report.

For the chairman of the Commission, who is a former Supreme Court justice and is versed in the legality of the situation, the non-publication may be an indication of the president's respect for the courts. The Commission, as established, also allows the government to reserve the right to publish a report if and when it is not politically expedient. Thus, a key debate regarding the report in post-HRVIC Nigeria concerns the reasons for the lack of publication. Is it legal or political? Whether legally or politically inhibited, can the non-publication of a truth and reconciliation report be justified? Perhaps this is where the Weberian maxim, noted in chapter one, informs the debate. If the president withholds the report in obedience to the courts, a decision possibly buttressed by the concern regarding the volatility of its impact, his action may be deemed to arise out of the moral parameters that place his burden of responsibility above his convictions. On the other hand, with the widespread public pressure for the release of the report, it not clear that his responsibility should not be to carry out the will of the society.[47]

Reflecting on public perception contemporary to the Commission's sittings, an article in *Today* reads:

> The public mood in the country is vengeful against the known and unknown violators of the people's rights. People, therefore, expect the Oputa Commission to unravel the mysteries, provide the answers, or the missing links, right the many wrongs of the past, and thus, heal the wounds.[48]

These public expectations of the Commission were ambitious and precipitated the chairman's response at the time, which he still maintains, that the Commission is part of a process that offers "Nigerians the opportunity to unravel their past, discuss it, embark on genuine reconciliation, and move ahead as a cohesive nation."[49] As such, the HRVIC was not a discrete event that would solve the problems and heal the wounds wrecked by Nigeria's violent past. It is only a starting point of a wider reconciliation process.

Public views were polarized by the stagnation of this process. Some argued that the HRVIC did its work and need not provide any reports, since the public was privy to the sitting through the media. For Nigerians who argue this position, the HRVIC served as the mechanism for hearing all sides. The responsibility of drawing conclusions now resides with the public. The Commission served simply as a mechanism for airing the past, allowing the public to acquit or convict accused perpetrators on an individual basis. For them, the issue of punishment and rewards are superfluous and unrealistic in the current political context. For others, the lack of a report is the proof that the Commission was President Obasanjo's personal publicity stunt, where he aimed to imitate the transitional approach of former South African President Mandela as a 'reconciling' leader who emerged after being imprisoned by an unpopular and oppressive regime.[50] Therefore, the Nigerian HRVIC was, ultimately, a hollow mimicry of the South African TRC as Nwankwo reflects:

> The Oputa Panel, a mocking ghost of South Africa's Truth and Reconciliation panel, sounds nice in Nigeria for Nigerian drama, an all too familiar drama regarding the feared and stony way toward truths that are constructive. That panel and what Nigerians are doing with it in relation to the bigger drama of reparation in South Africa, in the House of Mandela, suggests and points at a penchant for the meaningless pantomime, the comic relief in the fearful fight to flee from the real devils inside us.[51]

For one of the members of the Commission, the public is largely indifferent. He argues that "it is weird that not one Nigerian citizen or newspaper raised the issue of the unfinished Commission during the elections of 2003. The problem is that Nigerians know what it takes to get from A-B. Whether they are willing to do it is the question."[52] In this regard, he questions the genuineness of the Nigerian government's justification for not releasing the report as due to the court's ruling. He also questions the lack of initiative on the part of the public suggesting that they could sue the government and through the courts compel the government to release the report. Third, Father Kukah also questions both the absence of demanding political constituencies who do not demand accountability from their representatives and the silence of the legislative institutions over the official publication of the report.

Most people, including those who criticize the government for the non-publication of the report, acknowledge that the Commission succeeded in many ways. Indeed, one of the biggest successes of the Commission is the public consensus that the HRVIC provided a cathartic airing process for Nigerians. The Commission provided a space for people, victims and perpetrators, 'perceived victims and perpetrators alike', to speak and be heard. In some respects, the HRVIC broke the culture of silence. It opened a forum for debate on how to effectively deal with specific issues assailing the country and what the foundations for a new Nigeria should entail. Whether the forums remain open and viable will depend the interactions of individuals and their parliamentary representatives, as well as intellectuals and scholars at large. Additionally, there has been, as noted before a public condemnation and thus culpability that is now associated with those that refused to appear before the Commission.

HRVIC WITHOUT A REPORT

If the failures of the Commission outweigh its successes, then we cannot speak of the Commission *as* a success even though we might speak *of* its successes. As much as Nigerians have engaged in this process and are positive about the work of the HRVIC, the true effectiveness of the Commission in a general context is questionable without an official publication of its reports. As Brahms states,

> The commission's final report is its legacy. It is a summary of its key findings. Patterns of abuse are outlined. Most importantly, the commission's report provides recommendations for rebuilding society . . . In order to have maximum impact on society, the report should be widely disseminated. It seems unlikely that a truth commission can be considered a success if its findings are not made public. It is important that the entire population has access to the findings to better understand the trauma they have experiences. If a report is kept out of the public view, it will raise questions about the government's role in the violence.[53]

Even those who see the Commission as a success precede the positive judgment with the separation of the Commission from the executive arm of government that established it and that is responsible for publishing the report and implementing its recommendations. This position is not convincing in evaluating the HRVIC both as a truth commission and as a justice mechanism.

First and foremost, the HRVIC was unquestionably a truth commission by virtue of its elements. It was a temporary body, officially sanctioned, authorized, or empowered by the state to investigate a pattern of abuse of human rights violations over a set period of time that was in the past.[54] According to Popkin and Roht-Arriaza, truth commissions have four main goals, which are to create an authoritative record of what happened; provide a platform for victims to tell their stories and obtain some form of redress; recommend legislative, structural or other changes to avoid repetition of past abuses; and establish who was responsible and provide a measure of accountability.[55]

The HRVIC did provide an authoritative record. However, it is not officially in the public domain. It provided a platform for victims to tell their stories, but without the publication of a report it is arguable whether victims have obtained some form of redress. Fraser argues that the presentation of the petition and the audience given by the HRVIC to the victim provided recognitive justice. The question remains whether it is still justice if such recognition is not made official, that is, can such justice be deemed to have occurred at the hearing irrespective of the subsequent status of the commission and its report? It would seem that the non acknowledgment by the government is telling the victim that "it never happened," thereby consolidating the habits of the past. Third, the HRVIC included recommendations in its report. Again, without the publication of the report, the motivation for the recommendations, which is to avoid repetition of past abuses, is nullified. Similarly, whether the HRVIC established the responsibility of perpetrators and provided a measure of accountability is impossible to measure without the publication of the report. In sum, without the publication of the report, it is hard to argue for the success of the HRVIC. However, given the context of Commission's present status, it will also be inaccurate to argue that the Commission was unsuccessful. Therefore, it is most appropriately an incomplete truth commission.

While it is necessary to argue for the implementation of the recommendations, an argument for the release of the report is distinct. In many of the situations where a truth commission has been successfully instituted, there have been controversies surround the implementation of the report. Not even the most successful of truth commissions, the TRC is excepted from this challenge. The implementation of recommendations raises questions of justice, while the publication of the report raises issues regarding the validity of the commission as a truth commission. Therefore, the validity of the Nigerian HRVIC may rest on the publication of the report.

Regarding the question of justice whether truth commissions are instituted to obtain truths about the past so as to produce an institutionalized account of the past[56] or attempt to reduce the myths in circulation upon which notions of the 'other' are built,[57] it cannot be said to have achieved anything but the most minimal form of justice if it is unable to provide society with the documentation that reevaluates the past and promises a new future in light of that reevaluation. Without an official report and subsequent implementation of the recommendations, the goal of restoring social relationships remains a wish. The restoration of social relations through conflict resolution, as discussed in chapter one, lessens the likelihood of such conflicts recurring in the same way. Therefore, the report of a commission, which includes the compilation of the emotional and historical wounds of the nation and the recommendations for healing those wounds, is almost sacrosanct. Once any responsible government commits its society to a truth commission process, the implementation of the recommendations for obstructing the possibility of the wounds being inflicted again is necessary, even if not sufficient, for a 'new era' government that claims a moral mission to deal with the past for the sake of the future. While it can be argued that a government can implement recommendations without an official release of the report, the transparency of the government in implementing the recommendations can only be measured by the publication of the report so that the public can hold the government accountable. As such, the transparency and accountability of the government is contingent on the publication of the HRVIC report and the government's White Paper on the report.

CONCLUSION

As noted earlier, South Africa's report was no less controversial than Nigeria's at the dawn of its publication. The African National Congress and former President de Klerk both filed legal suits to try to halt publication and excise sections pertaining to them.[58] Neither of these cases halted the publication of the report, though de Klerk won an interdict to remove the sections pertaining to him. These cases were heard on October 29, 1998, and decided on because the publication was due later that month. The Court's decisions were made three hours before the time of presentation, so as to ensure that the Commission's process was completed.[59] The resolution of the controversy surrounding the TRC report seemed to be because the judges in charge of the case and President Mandela saw those cases as, not necessarily insignificant but, not more important than the South African nation-building problem as a whole. The importance of the report as the collective memory of South Africans was made primary. The publication of the report was also urgent, as it marked the commitment of the government to implement the recommendations of the TRC. Once publicized, the debates then revolved around the practicality and suitability of the report and recommendations as a foundation for reconciliation, and the speed of implementation of the recommendations. Only then is a truth commission's onus as part of a reconciliation and justice process of a nation fulfilled.

In Nigeria, Justice Oputa, the Chairman of the Commission, accepted the legal claim that justified the government's non-publication of the report. However, Father Kukah, another member of the Commission, saw it as politically motivated. Whether the reasons are legal or political, it can only be inferred that the Nigerian government did not place much importance on the report as a collective memory of Nigerians, so as to put the interest of all Nigerians above any individual's, institution's, or group's interests. Since the HRVIC was highly significant to the society, it is apparent that there are available remedies to get around the decision of the Supreme Court, if it indeed prohibits the government from publishing the report. Yet, years after the completion of the report, the government as well as the parliament, who can ratify the report of the commission, do not seem committed to the HRVIC's contribution to helping create a more just society in Nigeria. The controversies that plagued the HRVIC during its existence dim in light of the absence of its official report. It remains a tragedy to the Nigerian people and may come to be serve as a standard for judging the transitional status of the Obasanjo government.

Perhaps the accumulation of truths, fair hearings, and arguably therapeutic spaces for the peoples' voices were indeed achieved in the Nigerian case, thus dealing with the past. However, an official publication of the report and the White Paper, which includes the means to reconciliation and the structures to reestablish equality in social relations and prevent the recurrence of past violations, have been withheld. This also effectively aborts the institutionalization of *lessons learned for the future*. In this light, the HRVIC, remains incomplete. Despite its incomplete status, it is still possible to explore the extent to which it affected petitioners. The next chapter uses the Ohaneze petition as a case study for exploring the impact of the ideational and procedural components of the Commission.

NOTES

1. "Oputa is not Welcome Here," *Daily Trust*, March 13, 2001, Paper Copy; Dokin Karfe, "Oputa's Scale of Justice," *Gamji News* < http://www.gamji.com/NEWS1399.htm>, Accessed January 3, 2004; "How far can it go," *Vanguard*, July 7, 2001 <http://www.vanguardngr.com/news/articles/2001/July/07072001/f4070701.htm>, Accessed January 3, 2004; Chimalum Nwankwo, "In The House of Mandela: A Silly Cry for Reparations," *USAAfricaOnline*, 2001 < http://www.usafricaonline.com/chimalum.mandela.html>, Accessed January 3, 2004.
2. Father Matthew Kukah, Member of the Human Rights Violations Investigation Commission, interview by author, Cambridge, Mass., August 15, 2003.
3. See Appendix D.

4. See Appendix B and C. Compare the list of Commissioners in the June mandate (Appendix B) and in the October mandate (Appendix C).

5. See Appendix D.

6. Chief Eze-Ozogbu, Chairman of Ohaneze Ndi Igbo, interview by author, Enugu, Nigeria, September 9, 2003; Chief Dappa-Biriye, Chairman of the South-South People's Conference, interview by author, Port Harcourt, Nigeria, 11 September 2003; General IBM Haruna (rtd), Member of the Arewa Consultative Forum and Signatory and Chief Witness to the Arewa Petition, interview by author, Abuja, Nigeria, September 19, 2003.

7. Karfe, "Oputa's Scale of Justice."

8. Mrs. Chinwe Uwandu, Lead Counsel for the Human Rights Violations Investigation Commission, interview by author, New Haven, Connecticut, August 26, 2003.

9. Compare Appendix B and C.

10. Justice Chukwudifu Oputa, Chairman of the Human Rights Violations Investigation Commission, interview by author, Oguta, Nigeria, September 12, 2003.

11. Oputa, Chukwudifu, "The Struggle for a United Nigeria," Unpublished.

12. Chukwudifu Oputa, "On the Human Rights Violations Investigation Commission," Unpublished.

13. Uwandu, interview; *Today*, Jan 2–8, 2000.

14. Kukah, interview; *Today*, Jan 2–8, 2000.

15. Kukah, interview; Oputa, interview.

16. *Today*, Jan 2–8, 2000.

17. See Appendix C

18. Oputa, interview.

19. Oputa, interview.

20. Oputa, interview.

21. See Kirk-Greene (1971); Chukwudifu Oputa, "Professionalism, Shintoism, Loyalty, Allegiance and Patriotism," Unpublished; *Today*, Jan 2–8, 2000.

22. Chukwudifu Oputa, "Composite Ruling on the Refusal of some Ex-Presidents and other Top Government Functionaries to attend and Testify at the Proceedings of the Human Rights Violations Investigation Commission," Unpublished.

23. Oputa, "Composite Ruling," 11.

24. Ifi Amadiume and Abdullahi An-Na'im, "Introduction: Facing Truth, Voicing Justice" in *The Politics of Memory: Truth, Healing, and Social Justice*, ed. Ifi Amadiume and Abdullahi An-Na'im (London and New York: Zed Books 2000), 10.

25. Omo Omoruiyi, "Refocusing the Oputa Commission (2) the Military," *Niger Delta Congress* <http://www.nigerdeltacongress.com/rarticles/refocusing_the_oputa_commission%202.htm>, Accessed Dec 18 2003.

26. "Oputa is not Welcome Here," *Daily Trust*, March 13, 2001, Paper Copy; Haruna, interview.

27. Kukah, interview.

28. Uwandu, interview.

29. "The Cleric as an Activist: Interview with Father Matthew Hassan Kukah," *Guardian*, September 7, 2003, Paper Copy.

30. Oputa, interview.

31. Oputa, interview; Kukah, interview; Uwandu, interview.
32. Oputa, interview.
33. Oputa, interview; Kukah, interview; Uwandu, interview.
34. Oputa, interview; Kukah, interview; Uwandu, interview.
35. Kukah, interview.
36. Uwandu, interview.
37. Oputa, interview.
38. Uwandu, interview.
39. Chandra Lekha Sriram, *Confronting Past Human Rights Violations, Justice vs Peace in Times of Transition* (New York: Frank Cass, 2004), 46.
40. Greg Grandin, "The Instruction of Great Catastrophe: Truth Commissions, National History, and State Formation in Argentina, Chile and Guatemala," *The American Historical Review* 110, no. 1(2005): 3.
41. Oputa, interview.
42. Oputa, interview.
43. Oputa, interview.
44. Uwandu, interview.
45. The author saw the report, titled, *Synoptic Overview of HRVIC Report, Conclusions and Recommendations (Including Chairman's Foreword)*, in the custody of one of the petitioners interviewed, who showed it to me and admitted to owning it. He told me that the report was in the public library and promised to give me his copy to peruse only if I did not find a copy in the library. When I returned to him after my library visit as agreed, he did not give me his copy nor did he comment any further. I could not ascertain the source from which he had obtained the report. At the time of publication, the report had been officially released by civil society but not officially by the government.
46. *Fawehinmi vs. Babangida (2003) 12 WRN 1 (2003) NWLR (PT 808) 604.*
47. At the time of writing, the report has been unofficially released by a couple of civil society organizations and it has thus far, not engendered any significant cleavages or dissension among the Nigerian public. That is not to say that an official release would consequently have the same non violent impact. Perhaps, those against the release of the publication are silent, content in the reality that the unofficial publication does not have any legal or otherwise effective force or impact on Nigeria.
48. *Today*, Jan 2–8, 2000.
49. Oputa, interview.
50. Karfe, "Oputa's Scale of Justice."
51. Nwankwo, "In The House of Mandela: A Silly Cry for Reparations."
52. Kukah, interview.
53. Eric Brahm, "Truth Commissions," *Beyond Intractability*, June 2004 <http://www.beyondintratability.org/essay/truth_commissions/>, Accessed January 29 2007.
54. Priscilla B. Hayner, "Fifteen Truth Commissions–1974 to 1994: A Comparative Study," *Human Rights Quarterly* 16, no. 4 (1994).
55. Quoted in Brahm, "Truth Commissions," 6.
56. Priscilla B. Hayner, "Fifteen Truth Commissions," 607.

57. Stephen Landsman, "Accountability for International Crime and Serious Violations of Fundamental Human Rights: Alternative Responses to Serious Human Rights Abuses: Of Prosecution and Truth Commissions," *59 Law and Contemporary Problems* 81 (1996).

58. Martin Meredith, *Coming to Terms, South Africa's Search for Truth* (New York: Public Affairs, 1999).

59. Meredith, *Coming to Terms*, 302–305.

Chapter Three

A Case Study: The Ohaneze Petition and the Arewa Response

Chapter two presented an overview of how the HRVIC unfolded as a truth commission in general. Though the report of the HRVIC has not been published by the government, the live media coverage of its proceedings made it possible for the HRVIC process to still impact the Nigerian socio-political landscape. The Ohaneze petition is a petition that presented important political and historical conflicts before the HRVIC and will be used in this chapter, with the notable response that it generated, to examine the way in which politics and history interacted with the HRVIC.

THE CONTEXT FOR THE OHANEZE PETITION

The Ohaneze petition was the only petition that situated its testimony within the context of three very important events in Nigeria's history: the 1966 coups, the pogroms, and the civil war. This petition engendered petitions from other ethno-political groups, as well as the Arewa response, which was not a petition but a defense against the accusations that it felt were leveled against the members of the ethno-political group it represented. Apart from military cases, the Ohaneze petition recorded the largest number of witnesses. As stated by the lead counsel for the Commission, "It was one of the highlights of the public sittings because it generated what looked like a mini national conference in Nigeria."[1]

Ohaneze Ndi Igbo is the largest ethno-political organization that claim to speak for the Igbos of southeastern Nigeria. It was founded in 1978 after the Obasanjo military regime lifted the ban on political organizations and associations.[2] Ohaneze was patterned after the pre-independence Igbo State Union founded by Nnamdi Azikiwe to outline and work towards the development goals of the Igbos and their region.[3] Other Igbo organizations affiliated included with Ohaneze are the Igbo Youth Movement and the traditional rulers' council.[4] Additionally, the organization occasionally collaborates with the state governors of Igbo southeastern states.[5] Ohaneze allows for both formal and informal membership, which translates into 'non-active membership by virtue of birth.'[6]

Ohaneze's petition to the HRVIC was mainly designed to present an account of the wrongs it asserts were perpetrated against the Igbos from 1966 through 1999. The organization affirms that it did not necessarily believe in the good intentions of the government but in the good intentions of the HRVIC.[7] From the Commission's terms of reference, Ohaneze concluded that the Commission's work was primarily to find the truth of controversial events in Nigeria's history.[8] Thus, its goal became "to make Nigerians and the Commission aware of what happened, and the main crux of the petition was to show that the Igbos did not cause the coup of January 15, 1966."[9] Though the petition hinged on exonerating the Igbos from blame for the first Nigerian coup, its main grievance was the post-civil war marginalization of the Igbos.[10] Marginalization was extremely detrimental to the development of the Igbo region, and this, the organization argued, has long been wrongly justified by the claim that the January 15th coup was an Igbo coup aimed at Igbo political and military domination of the rest of the ethnic groups in the country. The anti-Igbo pogroms of 1966 and the counter coup of 1966 were seen as a response to the January coup and these responses culminated in the Nigerian-Biafran War of 1967–1970.

The Reconciliation, Rehabilitation, and Reconstruction Programme of the post war era was a government effort to underline General Gowon's "no victor, no vanquished" declaration at the end of the war.[11] However, the Ohaneze petition presented evidence to show that many government policies indicated a victor's justice despite the 'no victor, no vanquished' campaign. An example of this incongruity was the implementation of a financial policy that disallowed former Biafrans from gaining access to personal funds that were in Nigerian banks before the war. Rather, a standard sum of 20 pounds per bank client was made available regardless of the amount of money in the account.[12] Consequently, many people who had belonged to the short-lived Biafra lost a significant amount of wealth in Nigerian pounds. Indeed, most Nigerians believe that Biafra lost the war and the Nigerian government did not manifestly show them otherwise. The sentiment from anti-Biafra Nigerians was that a section of the country that attempts secession cannot seek to be rewarded from having lost in its attempts.[13] Rather, the government's refraining from punishing the executors of such an attempt is evidence of its benevolence.[14]

Nigeria's first coup, the pogroms, and the civil war still remain controversial. Contemporary ethnic insurgencies often invoke sentiments of injustice that many Igbos believe began with the pogroms of 1966. Without any far-reaching formal inquiry into the events of 1966, the incidents of the pogroms, for example, have remained beyond the reach of judicial process. For Ohaneze, the HRVIC was the necessary mechanism for the resolution of this past and 'enduring' conflict.

THE OHANEZE PETITION AND THE AREWA RESPONSE

As previously stated, the Ohaneze petition identified key violations of human rights that were denied any judicial investigation. These violations were not controversial in terms of the reality of these events but in terms of the perception of culpability and accountability of the actual or alleged perpetrators. These cases ranged from distant incidents, such as the Asaba Massacre of 1967, where whole villages were evacuated and their males killed and buried in mass graves, to more recent ones like the murder of Gideon Akaluka in 1994. Gideon was an Igbo man who lived in northern Kano state. He reportedly came back from work to hear that his wife was detained at a police station for using a loose leaf of the Koran lying in the dirt to wipe their child's bottom. On getting to the station to ascertain what had occurred, he was detained in place of his wife. On the evening of the next day, a mob came into his cell, beheaded him and paraded his head on a stick around the streets of Kano City.[15] Ohaneze's petition not only brought these cases under public scrutiny through a commission of inquiry but also highlighted the injustice of a society that had ignored these events for so long. As Father Kukah stated:

> The struggle against injustice has been with us a long time, and the highest expression of that injustice is the civil war. No sincere policies were established to actualize the elimination of those injustices, and Ohaneze drew attention to that. To have a commission deal with issues of a war 40 years after it was fought shows that the issues still persist.[16]

Ohaneze's petition presented the most comprehensive account of injustices meted out to members of the ethno-geographic region that it represents. The petition outlined issues that began and were contextualized in the ultimate complaint of marginalization. All instances of violations were organized under the following headings:

> Injustices and atrocities immediately before the civil war (1966–1967), the injustices and atrocities during the civil war (1967–1970), atrocities and

disempowerment immediately after the civil war (1970 to mid-seventies), and atrocities and disempowerment from the mid-seventies to date.[17]

The injustices and atrocities of the civil war were not given significant attention in terms of addressing the marginalization of the Igbos. Events within the war were debatably seen as necessary evils of an armed conflict that was consciously entered into, despite the claim by both sides that they had no choice. Thus, accusations regarding the war focused on accusations regarding Nigeria's flouting of the regulations of the United Nations Geneva Convention on the conduct of war.

The preamble to Ohaneze's account of injustices reveals one of the key problems to presenting a collective petition. The preamble states,

> The republican spirit of Ndi Igbo and their individual drive, expressing itself in a flair for fair competition in all spheres, encouraged them to exercise their citizenship rights all over Nigeria. The endeavours of Ndi Igbo, like those of other Nigerian citizens, were taking place in an atmosphere (so we thought) of brotherly debates and differences in our fledgling multi-ethnic democracy. But Ndi Igbo soon began to notice sinister stains in the responses of some national leaders to their differences with Ndi Igbo. Public statements of leaders of ruling political groups in Northern and Western Nigeria began to betray a disposition to extermination or total expulsion of Ndi Igbo as their acceptable solution of what they now saw as the Igbo problem. Speeches of Northern Nigeria Ministers, as recorded in Hansard of March 1964, and the anti-Igbo incitements in a booklet, UPGAISM, published by Western Government (1965) portrayed the new mood. This mood found a ready platform for explosion in January 15, 1966 coup d'état. The coup was falsely projected as an Igbo plot and used as a rallying cry to mobilize Northern Nigeria and some parts of the rest of the Federation to advance a genocidal plot against Ndi Igbo. The fiction and falsehood of [an] Igbo coup has long been admitted by some of the major actors in that episode, for example, Lt. Gen. T.Y Danjuma in Nigerian Civil War 1967–1970 edited by Major-General H.B. Momoh P.373.[18]

Thus, from the outset the petition presented an "us" versus "them" Manichean society. The collective petition in this sense detracted from the truth-telling by politicizing it. Had the preamble simply stated that Ohaneze as ethnicity would detail the stories of their particular experience of human rights violations, the sentiments that it generated may have still been one of defense but one that would speak directly to the accounting of those stories. As such, the preamble to the Arewa response was no more reconciliatory than the Ohaneze's introduction to its petition. While, the Arewa organization sent in its response because it felt "the need to put some records straight and the desire to encourage reconciliation and forgiveness,"[19] it states,

> It is an undisputed fact that the January 15, 1966 murders were part of an IGBO PROJECT which may have started in 1960, but conceived since the 1940s . . . Because of their nature of being overbearing, unduly aggressive, ethnocentric and inward looking. They had after 1960 Nigeria's Independence one AMBITION left to be realized and that was federal political power.[20]

The lack of acknowledgement of complicity makes it difficult for warring partners to confess to wrongdoing in order to reconcile. Ohaneze's inability to understand why the theory of Igbo domination in the January 15th coup, however false,[21] found credibility reflects a lack of self-examination. It is a fact that over 80 percent of the core planners of the coup were of Igbo background and over 80 percent of the casualties of the coup were of non-Igbo background.[22] It is a fact that the most revered traditional and religious ruler of the group that Arewa claims to represent was killed in that coup.[23] Therefore, even if the motivations of the coup were more about destroying neocolonial ills than they were about ethnic issues, the unachieved but intended results dim in light of factual events. A successful transition might have been acclaimed. However, the failure of the coup leaders to assume power only relegates the January 15, 1966, coup to the negative position of being the precursor of the culture of military coups and military rule in Nigeria. Consequently, the continuing defense, if not support, for the Nzeogwu coup in January 15, 1966, can only be seen as protection of one's own group. Arewa's response was no different. Without any acknowledgment of the violations detailed in Ohaneze's petition, it began with the rehearsed story of the January 15th coup as an Igbo coup. The organizations' creation of an 'us' versus 'them' sentiment as it aired on television seemed to run counter to the spirit of a truth commission that aimed at reconciliation. On the other hand, the HRVIC may have served the purpose of providing a space for these perceptions to confront, each other and to air the real hostilities that operates in ethnic interactions, as denoted by the preambles.

This interaction also indicates that Nigeria's HRVIC may have been better structured if it were aimed at hearing individual stories and ascertaining individual rather than collective responsibility. Even a collective issue such as the pogroms or genocidal policies of the war would have been more powerfully told by individual experiences. This is particularly relevant, given the status of ethnic identities and the historically negative consequences of blaming the entirety of an ethnic group rather than the particular perpetrators of a crime. Ohaneze did not distinguish between organizing Igbos, whose rights had been violated to present their petition, and presenting an Igbo petition. The problematic nature of this petition can be understood with an example of a hypothetical ANC petition encompassing all violations against Africans under apartheid. The South African TRC found violations, victims, and perpetrators on all sides. Collective petitions can undermine an attempt to evince the complexities, nuances, and contradictions of conflict. It also undermines the goal of creating national identities for both victims and the watching public. The petitions thus reinforced one of the biggest structural problems in Nigeria: the conceptualization and contextualization of incidents in terms of ethnic or religious identities. This lack of understanding was not corrected by the Commission's counsels who sorted out the claims that were eligible as petitions of gross violations of human rights. As such, Ohaneze's petition, while valid vis-à-vis the experiences that it called up and valued for tearing open one of the main aspects of Nigerian life that is cloaked in silence and myths, also heralded the use of the Commission by other ethno-political groups as a means of reconstructing history for the purpose of political posturing and spoils politics.

As noted earlier, the response of the Arewa Consultative Forum, the counterpart of Ohaneze that claims to speak for the north, to the Ohaneze petition not only reinforced the errors of Ohaneze but compounded them. Most significantly, the acceptance of its response by the Commission broke some of the Commission's regulations and further increased the potency of ethnic dynamics by which all players, including the commissioners, were then bound. The HRVIC set a deadline for when all petitions were to be received. Under the HRVIC procedures, any accused person or group mentioned in a petition was summoned to give their perspective on the submitted petitions. In the case of Ohaneze, the accused ranged from the government to specific individuals. In accordance with the regulations of the Commission, Arewa, as an entity, was not summoned because it was not mentioned in the petition. Yet Arewa pressed for representation before the Commission so as to respond to the Ohaneze petition, since some of the accused were, by virtue of birth if not direct affiliation, members of the ethno-political group it represented.[24] While this is not procedurally correct, it may have generally been substantively right to allow the participation of Arewa, as they were also stakeholders in the re-establishment of Nigeria's social relations as discussed in chapter one. The flexibility of practical justice allows for it. The chairman of the Commission argued that in order to uphold the virtue of fair hearing, the Commission was compelled to hear Arewa's response. Underlying this reasoning was the fact that the chairman, being an Igbo, could not effectively deny Arewa the opportunity to state its case despite not meeting the requirements for being heard. Any such act would have brought the impartiality and legitimacy of the Commission into question.

The allowance made for Arewa opened the door to any person or group who felt the need to defend any accusation or name mentioned in the petitions that were picked for public hearing. It turned this part of the HRVIC from a truth-telling space to a forum for continuing articulation of broader, group-based historical and political grievances. The Arewa response not only introduced what became petitions of defense, they also introduced cross-examinations during the public hearings. This introduction of cross-examination limited the safe space that the Commission was supposed to create for real and perceived victims. It also affected the nature of the public hearings, as it introduced undertones of a courtroom and often turned the HRVIC hearings into a non-judicial litigation of actual and perceived ethnic grievances.

The Arewa response presented a point-by-point response to each era of injustice that Ohaneze outlined. In most cases, Arewa presented a different perspective on history as presented by Ohaneze, though historical claims of the coups, the progroms, and civil war were not contradictory to those made by Ohaneze. For example, on the issue of political domination by the North, the response explains that "The domination of political power by the North was as a result of numerical strength."[25] It also acknowledges the corrupt nature of past leaders and argue that such leaders are not found only within the North but are found in the South as well. It points out that the residence of political leadership in the North does not translate into greater development opportunities for the North, given the 'selfishness and shortsightedness' of these past leaders.[26]

Indeed, the preponderance of northerners in Nigeria's leadership has not translated into development opportunities for the region. However, rather than petitioning against those that they acknowledged were and are a corrupt and culpable elite in defense of the common "Northerner," Arewa hoped to deflect the culpability of these elites arguing that such leaders were not peculiar to the North. Ohaneze's position differed from this stance, because Ohaneze did not defend the elite of its region but the ordinary Nigerian who has been victimized by the elite. However, Ohaneze's petition omitted to implicate its own corrupt elite in the victimization of the Igbos and positioned the ordinary Igbo victim largely against past governments that were dominated by the elite of a different ethno-political group. Thus, the possibility of individual or class identity at the national level was regarded as secondary to the maintenance of intra-group solidarity among these ethno-political associations.

Furthermore, the issue of numerical strength, which Arewa argued as a justification of prolonged leadership of Nigeria by northern elites, falsely indicates that Nigeria has experienced consistent democratic regimes where the populace votes leaders in. Such argument for numerical strength is perhaps only relevant to the first republic and short-lived second republic.[27] Even so, Ohaneze's cases were largely against military regimes. Some of the controversial cases that the two groups tackled were the coups of 1966, the pogroms, and the civil war.

THE COUP OF JANUARY 15, 1966

Ohaneze presented the coup of January 1966 as the origin of and as a false justification, for most human rights violations against the Igbos from 1966 to 1999. While it saw the coup as a popular non-ethnic coup that sought to deal with the problems of the First Republic, Arewa saw the coup as both ethnically motivated and the source of illegitimate military regimes in Nigeria. Arewa states,

> Nigeria's march towards military rule and incessant political instability has [*sic*] been the direct consequence of the actions of a cabal of military officers largely of Igbo extraction. Aside from introducing selective violence and murder as means to solving political problems, they took the first critical actions to uproot the democratic culture and consensus upon which the Nigerian Federation was built when they overthrew the elected government of Northern Nigeria on the 15th of January, 1966 through a mutiny and subsequently of a Federation, and thereafter imposed a Unitary government on Nigeria.[28]

Arewa asserted that Igbos, despite "their dominance in most aspects of public and private commercial life," sought more power.[29] This belief that the coup was an Igbo coup was borne out of realities surrounding the coup. The coup casualties were mostly non-Igbos and included key leaders from the North. While the Igbo Nigerian President had just left the country, the Hausa-Fulani Prime minister had just returned from his religious pilgrimage and was killed in the coup. Furthermore, rather than a restoration of law and order, the Igbo commanding general of the army took over the reins of government and began to make fundamental constitutional changes through military decrees.[30]

Ohaneze rebutted the accusation that the coup was an Igbo coup, as the Igbos did not have any incentive to topple the 1966 government. Ohaneze stated:

> If the Igbo race is credited with any intelligence, one would ask; 'what sort of power or position do the Igbos want in 1966, which they did not have, to warrant a conspiracy by way of a coup plot to achieve'?[31]

Given that, in 1966, President Nnamdi Azikiwe, Senate President Nwafor Orizu and the Commander of the Nigerian Army, Lieutenant General Ironsi were all Igbos, the argument for political domination as the motive of the coup is unconvincing. The military intervention that subdued the coup was led by a group of Igbo officers.[32] As such, Igbos quelled an 'Igbo' coup. Ohaneze also stated that both the president and prime minister were made aware of the impending coup. The president chose to leave the country while the prime minister remained.[33]

Despite examination and cross-examination of witnesses, no resolution could be reached, and the Commission was left with the duty of deciding what the official truth of the January coup would be. It is highly doubtful that the decision of the Commission will change the long-held perspectives of the two organizations, since those perspectives are part of standard politicized histories that define the identities of the organizations.

THE POGROMS OF 1966

The pogroms of 1966 were presented within the Ohaneze petition as events engendered by the January 1966 coup. According to the petition, "Igbo citizens in Northern Nigeria were massacred in three waves of pogrom in the most sadistic and inhuman methods that made Jewish holocaust appear like mercy killings. Approximately 50,000 Igbos were slaughtered."[34] Some of the inhuman methods of slaughter were recorded in affidavits of eyewitnesses, some of which were compiled in the Ohaneze petition.

The petition asserts that the pogrom accounts offer just a minute glimpse into the enormity of the event that eventually 'forced Igbos out of Nigeria.' In describing the pogrom, it states,

> The massacre of Igbo women and children who were deceived into flocking to railway stations in search of passenger trains to take them home, forcible collection of Igbo female students from schools and herding of them into leper colonies, to be defiled by lepers; the slaughtering in the transit zone of Middle-Belt of Igbo refugees who managed to escape the wrath of far North; the refusal virtually of all Nigerians to give protection to any Easterner; the active involvement of law-enforcement agencies in the pogroms; and the exodus of 2 million people in flight from a country that has rejected them and that has offered them nothing but a mass grave. Indeed, the future of no future confronting Ndi Igbo at this time was symbolized by the fate of Igbo babies at the Kano railway holocaust.[35]

Ohaneze distinguished between the April/May pogrom and the September/October recurrence. It argued that even if they were to accept a justification of the first pogrom, the counter coup of July 1966 should have cancelled out the January coup. Thus, there was no justifiable reason for the second pogrom. Besides the justifiability of the pogroms, the petition did not seek to find out 'what happened.' Ohaneze argued that the organized nature of the events indicated that pogroms were not the consequence of a sudden irrational action by the mob, but it did not specifically seek to establish the truth of how these pogroms occurred, what specific truths were missing and who was accountable for them.

The HRVIC did not seem interested in making further inquiries either, as the legal counsel asserted that:

> Attempts to make inquiries into certain events, even in more recent ones than the pogroms, were met with a brick wall. The Commission made efforts to ascertain specific individual accountability for events like in the case of Gideon Akaluka. The Commission did try to probe in that direction and there was a limit to how far we could get and we could not quite get anything that was not really in the public domain in that particular case. And the chairman wanted to avoid the situation where we started pointing out individuals. In an attempt to individualize the issues, we might actually rake up things that could create even bigger problems. Sometimes, the chairman decided that we should discontinue further inquiries. He was the chairman and whatever he wanted done was done. So if he felt we were over reaching, he would sort of call us back.[36]

It would seem that the Commission was trying to uncover truth in a way that would not result in the eruption of violence around the country. Truth, as argued in chapter one, was functional.

It is possible that a situation that seemed advantageous to Ohaneze within the dynamics of ethnic politics, that is, its ethnic commonality with the Chairman of the Inquiry, in actuality limited the needed probing regarding some of Ohaneze's instances of human rights violations. The legal counsel affirmed that "the Ohaneze petition was a very sensitive petition for the chairman because he is an Igbo man and he had to be careful with his decisions on it."[37] On the other hand, the chairman of the Commission argued for the legality of the limitation in investigating the pogroms. He states that the commission "was not privileged to inquire further because the pogroms were mentioned as a response of the North to the alleged Igbo coup. Thus, it was not presented as an issue of human rights violation but in passing as evidence for anti-Igbo response of the North to the January coup."[38] As such, the narrative of the pogroms was reinterpreted as part of a narrative of historical marginalization and the truths surrounding them deemed a footnote of history. Perhaps, Soyinka's proposition in chapter one, that the magnitude of certain events propels them to a realm beyond the language of redress, only allowing for "purgation" and "quiescent stock-staking, an affirmation of existence in the present and a resolve in defense of unborn generations."[39] This may have been the case for the pogroms.

Ultimately, Ohaneze's human rights violations petition and the Commission's investigations of the same violations guided by the petition focused more on the crime of marginalization. In a response to the South African ANC argument for the consideration of their acts as acts of a just war, Archbishop Desmond Tutu stated that "Human Rights violations were human rights violations."[40] In this declaration he explained that searching for the justifications of the acts rather than ascertaining the "what happened" of an act so as to implement the "never again," was irrelevant. In Nigeria, the HRVIC seemed to do the opposite. It seemed that some human rights violations were seen as subjective and justifiable by the petitioners, and those instances did not necessitate further inquiry.

THE ASABA MASSACRE

The relevance of the civil war to the terms of reference of the Commission was contentious, as the war was seen in a different light from other events presented in the Ohaneze petition. The Asaba massacre, though an event that occurred during the civil war, is studied in the text because of a peculiarity that derives from its geopolitical standing during the civil war. Asaba was part of the Midwestern region of Nigeria and outside the Eastern region when the Eastern region seceded as Biafra on May 29, 1967. The military government of the mid-west had initially tried to stay out of the conflict declaring neutrality.[41] Yet mass graves are present-day evidence of the atrocious violations of human rights against the Asaba people during the Nigerian-Biafran civil war.

There are numerous speculations as to the reason why Asaba bore some of the worst atrocities of the Nigerian Civil War. Some argue that military officers of Northern origin felt vengeful towards the Mid-west as it was the home region of Major Nzeogwu, the January 15, 1966 coup leader who personally executed one of the most revered traditional rulers of the North, Sardauna of Sokoto.[42] Others argue that the Nigerian army saw Igbo inhabitants of Asaba, by virtue of being Igbo, as Biafrans and thus Biafran supporters. A witness who recounted the words of a Nigerian second lieutenant who oversaw one of the Asaba massacres affirms this claim. He stated: "He condemned all of us to death with this simple sentence: "I come from Chad but them born me from Adamawa, I hate all Ibos, you be Ibo therefore you must die."[43] Whatever the reason, the Asaba area "was one of the centers of mass killings. The soldiers lured out civilians into an open field to welcome them. In a premeditated plan, they sprayed the civilians with bullets, killing over 700 males."[44] A witness, who survived the shootings after his village was evacuated and the villagers were led to an open space, corroborated this account. He states,

> At the open space, they stopped and separated the men from the women and children. I was 15 years old, small for my age. I tried to stay with the women

> and children but I was forced back into the group of men. So I stayed near my brother Emma who was nineteen and held on to him. I looked around, and I saw that the troops had surrounded us with machine guns . . . There was pandemonium as we all fell on each other. The last I saw of my father was a bloody face. All I could hear was the rapid fire of machine guns and screams of anguish from my kinsmen who have been hit. Some of them who had been hit so badly stood up and begged the soldiers to kill them properly . . . I have lived for thirty-three years crying every night for my brothers and friends who died. I hope the pains will now cease.[45]

Even in the absence of the HRVIC report, Dr. Uriah's case is one of the success stories of the Commission, as he saw the petition as 'the space to finally tell' a story he had held on to for over three decades.[46] This is a great example of the recognitive justice that Fraser postulates. From his testimony, it would seem that Dr. Uriah's relief came with his opportunity to tell his story not just before the HRVIC but before a country who listened through radios and televisions. By this opportunity, his victimization was made real, and as Soyinka suggests, "acknowledged." Dr. Uriah was cross-examined by the Arewa counsel but the cross-examination did not last for long as the Chairman of the Commission seemed aggressive in answering questions aimed at Dr. Uriah. This was possibly to stave off the potential of a cross-examination that could have destroy the atmosphere of truth telling that the story generated and reduced it to some form of ethnic politicking.

OHANEZE'S PRAYERS

Ohaneze ended its petition with requests that it argued would bring some measure of healing for the Igbos as well as the Nigerian people as a whole. Ohaneze's remedies included financial compensations for bereaved and humiliated families in respect of the alleged murdered, the maimed, the raped, and the dehumanized; financial compensation for wrong dismissals from the civil service; financial compensation for the havoc of scorched earth policies; reversals of economic marginalization policy, and restitution where possible. Despite the lack of focus on the pogroms on who was accountable for the pogroms, the petition requested the trial of the pogroms' perpetrators.[47] Additionally, it requested the trial of war crime perpetrators.[48] Ohaneze summarized its requests by pointing to the two key needs of the group for healing. The first was a national apology by the government for all the injustices meted out to the Igbos throughout Nigeria's history.[49] The second was a request for an assurance of 'Ozoemena,' an Igbo phrase that means 'never again.'[50]

Making suggestions for how to move the nation forward, Ohaneze advanced a new agenda, not particular to itself, for addressing the constitutional foundations of the Nigerian Federation:

> Our Constitution must address more explicitly and unequivocally than it has done hitherto the foundational question of the character of our Federal union. Should Nigeria be a mosaic of self-reinforcing ethnic mini-sovereignties barely interacting horizontally but intensively engaged vertically in a cockpit fight for the largest loot from the center? Or, a dynamic multi-ethnic community purposefully evolving towards the end state of healthy national integration? It is surprising that our utterances and actions have shown that this basic choice has not been made after 40 years of togetherness.[51]

CONCLUSION

The truth of the January coup case was left to the commissioners to try to decipher. The issue of the pogrom and the 1966 coups did not regard the reality of those events but the process that brought them about. The Ohaneze contingent argued that the pogroms were organized as part of the marginalization efforts against the Igbos while the Arewa group responded that it was instead an emotive mob that took to the streets on three different occasions having been enraged by the political events of the time. In the Arewa argument, they ignored the widespread initiative and participation of soldiers in the pogrom of September-October 1967.[52]

While Dr. Uriah's story was one of the successes of the HRVIC, the ethnic petitions seemed fraught with politics. Ohaneze's excuses for the Nzeogwu coup, rather than acknowledgement of the wrongful act of toppling a democratic government, presented, if nothing else, a lack of empathy at the victimization of the other. Perhaps, if the individuals who had personally experienced victimization from the different ethnicities had been able to speak in the common space provided, the atmosphere generated by the ethnic petitions would have been different. At the end of the sittings, it would seem that despite the true horrors that befell millions of ordinary people in these key events, nothing further than the truths and myths already in the public domain had been obtained from the accounts and cross-examinations of witnesses. Rather, the solidification of collective ethnic responsibility that was engendered by the hearings threatened to make a mockery of the HRVIC and to undermine its ability to identify truth and promote reconciliation. More ethno-geographical organizations brought their responses to the Ohaneze and Arewa reports, making claims about their marginalization in the sharing of the nation's resources to the benefit of the three largest ethnic groups in Nigeria. It would seem that the Ohaneze petition had become a 'marginalization petition', along with the rest of the other ethnic petitions.

Ohaneze lawyers and representatives seemed content with such a conclusion. For them, their petition was public and prepared for posterity. The response of the government to their case was mostly important to them in terms of their charge of marginalization. They argued that they were realistic enough to realize that issues of the past have political significance in the contemporary Nigerian state, given that those past players are still relevant in the present political scene.[53] As such, a true national reconciliation with the past was merely a mirage in the current Nigeria.

With such a perspective, it would appear that the Ohaneze petitioners were not totally committed to the notion of reconciliation to the past as citizens of a nation but rather sought some form of reconciliation of their region's role in Nigeria's history. They sought, more pragmatically, to reconcile with a Federal government that was the primary accused but also the source of sought-after resources for their development needs. The Ohaneze members argued that reconciliation with any group or establishment was impossible without the publication of the report. Thus, following the Commission's hearings, they focused on self-reconciliation as an ethnic group to the violence wreaked on them. This manifested itself in events such as the remembrance of their dead who were killed in the civil war, pogroms, and other ethnic insurgencies to date. Among the Asaba, a committee was set up to work on the construction of a monument for those massacred in Asaba.[54] Despite the appropriateness of these intra-ethnic efforts, they cannot achieve the stabilization of the country as a whole. National stabilization is dependent on reconciliation at the inter-ethnic level.

The Arewa Forum saw Ohaneze's petition as the continuation of the civil war rather than a reconciliatory effort.[55] In its 'prayers,' it avers that in the spirit of forgiveness and reconciliation, the Commission should "ignore all claims of the Ohaneze petition which are baseless and unsubstantiated."[56] It would be optimistic to interpret this request of the organization as a wise prayer, which only advocates the ignoring of unproven facts. However, it would seem that the petition deemed issues regarding "acts done during the civil war, or acts connected with the war" as beyond the rights of Igbos to claim grievances.[57] Arewa, in the manner of Ohaneze, espoused the need for solutions to the violence and tensions that besiege Nigeria. However, just as with every other ethno-political petition, they were oblivious to their lack of empathy for the 'other.' This inability to empathize that is symptomatic of all the ethnic petitions points to the core of Nigeria's ethnic problems.

On the other hand, this very public interaction between the ethnic groups on these issues opened an uncharted public forum for the Nigerian public and some of the circulating myths became real for many people. Yet, the truth surrounding particular cases remained a mystery due to the reproduction of particular perspectives. With each petition reproducing perspectives, which selectively remember, interpret, and forget past events, it would seem that these ethno-political groups were merely engaged in familiar habits in the newly created truth and reconciliation space. To what extent the HRVIC can effect change in such a context is the question of the final chapter. However, before investigating the impact of the HRVIC, it is important to examine the unintended consequences of the HRVIC which help to reveal the realities of a truth commission.

NOTES

1. Mrs. Chinwe Uwandu, Lead Counsel for the Human Rights Violations Investigation Commission., interview by author, New Haven, Connecticut, August 26, 2003.
2. Chief Eze-Ozogbu, Chairman of Ohaneze Ndi Igbo, interview by author, Enugu, Nigeria, September 9, 2003.
3. Eze-Ozogbu, interview.
4. Eze-Ozogbu, interview.
5. Eze-Ozogbu, interview.
6. Eze-Ozogbu, interview.
7. Eze-Ozogbu, interview.
8. Eze-Ozogbu, interview.
9. Eze-Ozogbu, interview.
10. Eze-Ozogbu, interview.
11. See Kirk-Greene (1971), Obasanjo (1980).
12. Nneoma V. Nwogu, "Ethnic Revivalism: Recasting the Legacy of the Nigerian Civil War" (BA Thesis, Wellesley College, 2002); Ifi Amadiume, "Biafra and Intellectual Responsibility," in *The Politics of Memory: Truth, Healing and Social Justice*, ed. Ifi Amadiume and Abdullahi An-Na'im (London and New York: Zed Books 2000).
13. Father Matthew Kukah, Member of the Human Rights Violations Investigation Commission, interview by author, Cambridge, Mass., August 15, 2003.
14. Kukah, interview.
15. Uwandu, interview.
16. Kukah, interview.
17. Ohaneze Petition 1648 I.
18. Ohaneze Petition 1648 I, 3.
19. Arewa Response Ext. 64-1648 I, 4.
20. Arewa Response Ext. 64-1648 II, 7.
21. One of the coup plotters who is on non Igbo origin, in his book *Why we Struck*, recounted the story of how five idealist military men who were frustrated by the

magnitude of corruption in the country, took the law into their hands because they felt it was their civil and military duty to protect their country from the "enemy." Their goal was to take over the helm of political leadership and "vigilantly guide the country along the paths of democratic socialism." Olusegun Obasanjo, who is now the president corroborates this version in his book, *My Command,* arguing that the goal of the coup was "to establish a strong unified and prosperous nation, free from corruption and internal strife" (1980), 6.

22. See Madiebo (1980), Ademoyega (1981).

23. See Madiebo (1980), Ademoyega (1981).

24. General IBM Haruna (rtd), Member of the Arewa Consultative Forum and Signatory and Chief Witness to the Arewa Petition, interview by author, Abuja, Nigeria, September 19, 2003.

25. Arewa Response Ext. 64-1648 I, 7

26. Arewa Response Ext. 64-1648 I, 7.

27. See Post and Vickers (1973).

28. Arewa Response Ext. 64-1648 II, 3–4.

29. Arewa Response Ext. 64-1648 II, 3–4.

30. Arewa Response Ext. 64-1648 II, 7.

31. Final Address of the Ohaneze petition quoted in Oputa II, Unpublished.

32. Oputa, Chukwudifu, "The Struggle for a United Nigeria," Unpublished, 8.

33. Oputa, "The Struggle for a United Nigeria."

34. Ohaneze Petition 1648 I.

35. Ohaneze Petition 1648 I, 4. The fate of Ibo babies referred to in the above statement comes out of a story reprinted in the Ohaneze petition by an Igbo man who recounted his experience to a tribunal set up by the South eastern region in the aftermath of the war to document the experience of pogrom victims. He states: "It was announced over Kano Rediffusion Network that a passenger train would be leaving Kano for Eastern Region on 2nd of October (1966), and that all those wishing to travel should report on 1st of October at the Railway Station (due to the waves of pogroms of 1966—May 29, July 29, and September) . . . . . . Somebody emerged from under the big table on hearing me. It was Mr. Lekettey, a Ghanaian who apparently was hiding from the savage soldiers. He was my uncle and I his nephew. This strategy worked wonderfully, and when the soldiers heard us out, they shouted in unison, 'why have you been hiding? We don't want to kill Ghanaians. We are after Okpara's brothers. We are going to finish them off. They took us upstairs, where we saw more dead bodies, some of whom I recognised. Lekettey and myself gave them ten pounds for drink. They drank until 6.30 am the following morning, 2nd of October. These soldier had some harsh things to say about Okpara and Ibos: 'Okpara was their arch enemy who must be destroyed . . . All other Igbos must be destroyed.' At 7 a.m. that same Sunday morning, they asked Mr Lekettey and myself to get ready because they were going to show us how we have dealt with Okpara's brothers and sisters.' They took us to the Railway Station in an army landrover and there we saw a sight I would never like to see again till my dying day. Over 700 men, women, and children had been mowed down—they had been killed while they were waiting for a train to take them to our Region. A few of the children were still creeping over their dead

mothers, shouting, 'Mama, I am hungry; I want to drink.' Some were trying to suck their dead mothers' breasts . . ." (excerpt from the Ohaneze Petition 1648 I).

36. Uwandu, interview.

37. Uwandu, interview.

38. Justice Chukwudifu Oputa, Chairman of the Human Rights Violations Investigation Commission, interview by author, Oguta, Nigeria, 12 September 2003.

39. Wole Soyinka, "Memory, Truth and Healing" in *The Politics of Memory: Truth, Healing and Social Justice*, ed. Ifi Amadiume and Abdullahi An-Na'im (London and New York: Zed Books 2000), 35.

40. Martin Meredith, *Coming to Terms, South Africa's Search for Truth* (New York: Public Affairs, 1999), 211.

41. See Kirk-Greene (1971)

42. See Ademoyega (1981).

43. "I am from Chad [a country bordering Nigeria on the Northeast], but I was born in Adamawa [a Nigerian region, now a state, in the North]. I hate all Igbos. You are Igbo so you must die." Dr. Uriah, "Statement" obtained from Barrister Nduka-Eze, Counsel for the Asaba People during an interview by author, Lagos, Nigeria, September 25, 2003.

44. Ohaneze Petition 1648 II, 20.

45. Uriah, "Statement."

46. Uriah, "Statement."

47. Ohaneze Petition 1648 II, 50.

48. Ohaneze Petition 1648 II, 50.

49. Ohaneze Petition 1648 II, 50.

50. Ohaneze Petition 1648 II, 50.

51. Ohaneze Petition 1648 II.

52. See Kirk-Greene (1971).

53. Eze-Ozogbu, interview; Chief Mogbo, Lead Counsel for Ohaneze Ndi Igbo, interview by author, Enugu, Nigeria, September 15, 2003. Enugu, Nigeria.

54. Barrister Nduka-Eze, Counsel for the Asaba People, interview by author, Lagos Nigeria, September 25, 2003.

55. Arewa Response Ext. 64-1648 II, 4.

56. Arewa Response Ext. 64-1648 II, 35.

57. Arewa Response Ext. 64-1648 I, 23.

Chapter Four

The Politics of Unintended Consequences

INTRODUCTION

Often the outcome of a political process is determined by a combination of the active process of pursuing an ideal and the unintended consequences that derive from that pursuit. Given the political contentiousness of truth commissions, there is no guarantee that their outcome will be strictly guided by the motivations behind their establishment. The continuous engagement with society necessarily leads to a constant revision of the procedure by which the stated goal is achieved. The goals are themselves not impervious to change or questioning.

With respect to the South African TRC, the African National Congress, National Party, Inkatha Freedom Party, and Freedom Front all found problems with the final report and, consequently, publicly denounced parts of it.[1] The TRC caused internal conflicts within the party and government that set it up, based on contested notions of procedures and definitions.[2] The HRVIC was not an exception to the rule of unintended consequences. In fact, the lack of careful strategizing and process in its establishment arguably made it more vulnerable to unintended outcomes. These unintended outcomes did not only surface at the end of the sittings but crucially emerged during the course of the hearing process and affected the very proceedings of the Commission.

UNINTENDED DEVELOPMENTS

The intentions of the Obasanjo regime would seem apparent to a post-TRC continent that sees the benefits of truth commissions as a pragmatic approach to transitional politics. However, the abrupt setting up of the Commission in the context of an unanticipated and hurried transition to democracy provided rational foundations for critics of President Obasanjo's approach to human rights injustices in the country. As Nduka-Eze states,

> I do not believe that the Government was sincere in setting up the Oputa panel. It was intended to be a hogwash carried out due to the fashionability of truth commissions since South Africa's TRC. It is possible that they [government] did not realize that people would take it seriously but it was totally embraced unexpectedly and gathered momentum of its own. I say this also because if the government was truly committed to the work of the panel, the injunction case would have been adjudicated a long time ago.[3]

The idea that Obasanjo's intentions in the creation of the HRVIC may have been at best a political ploy emerged at the inception of the HRVIC and was debated in the public forums organized by the Commission in preparation for its assignment. One of the Commission's media consultants noted this skepticism in a national paper:

> Many are unsure and/or doubtful about the seriousness of the Commission and the government that set it up, and, perhaps, even suspicious of the motives behind the exercise. Repeatedly, questions were asked, about whether this whole exercise is not really intended as a diversion or a mere gimmick by the Obasanjo government; about whether the Commission will be any different from, and its final report and recommendations will not suffer the same fate as, many similar Commissions set up in the past; about whether the Commission really has the powers, and can be sufficiently free from government control and manipulation to do what it says it will do; about whether the government itself can muster enough will and courage to deal with some violators who may be in high places.[4]

These early doubts about the fate of the report, which have in retrospect proven valid, do not only rest their present justification on the delay which the government has allowed, even if by omission, on the adjudication of the injunction case.[5] Another signal for these concerns is the apparent intimacy between the President, who is a key defendant to the injunction case and Nigeria's former military ruler, General Ibrahim Babangida, who is the plaintiff in the injunction case. This intimacy is noted unofficially in the presence of the President's wife at a high profile wedding of General Babangida's daughter while the President was at the General Assembly meeting in New York, and officially in General Babangida's representation of the President on official engagements with other governments.[6]

Yet the publicity generated by the Commission and the credibility and initiative of the commissioners led to a public response that effected the expansion of the period to be investigated. The extension of the period also meant an expansion of the number of human rights violations to be covered, and the parameters of the Commission's mandate. These changes allowed for the formal accusation of President Obasanjo, the originator of the HRVIC, as a perpetrator of human rights violations during his military rule in the late 1970s. According to the media, this had the paradoxical effect of raising both public expectation and skepticism. In terms of expectation, the dramatic turn that transformed a president whose case for presidential eligibility was made partly on the basis of his victimization by the previous military regime to a past military leader who perpetrated human rights violations caught the interest of the public. The same public, now watching skeptically, waited to "see how the Oputa Commission would handle cases arising from the tenure of General Obasanjo, and whether this would just be another one of those inquiries whose reports and recommendations never see the light of day but end up on shelves gathering dust."[7]

Another consequence that arose from the expansion of the period to be investigated was the presentation of the Ohaneze petition. This petition and the other ethnic petitions and responses it engendered, positively used the HRVIC to transform some myths into truths, but more visibly used the forum as a tool for revitalizing sedimented ethnic identities as seen in chapter three. The wide media coverage of the HRVIC provided ethno-political groups with an immediate medium for circulating subjective political convictions through the retelling of history. The ethnic-based spoils politics of "who we are determines what we get" was thus replayed. In this process of the key elements of a truth and reconciliation commission, appropriate for Nigeria, which is to break down collective guilt to individual culpability in a society frayed with communal conflict, was frustrated. All the ethno-political groups deemphasized individual guilt and victimization and internal tensions so as to retain the primacy of collective identity. Since Ohaneze's petition situated the source of its core arguments in the events of the latter half of the 1960s, would the HRVIC have encountered ethnic politics to the degree that it did if the period had not been extended? Without the expansion of the relevant period for investigation, the politicization of the HRVIC would still have entailed ethnic debacles channeled through military politics or more recent 'ethnic' insurgences. As such, the constant presence of ethnic politics indicates the somewhat static nature of Nigerians' overall political memory and mentality. Perhaps then, the open confrontation with ethnic discord played out so publicly by the elite before the larger citizenry allows the public to engage with these issues more confidently in open spaces as well, thus, this open confrontation becomes a positive outcome.

The third consequence is the unwitting conversion of a public hearing into a trial-like space. This was due to a combination of the influence of the Chairman's professional background, the need to establish some form of legal legitimacy for the HRVIC in the absence of a secure legislative standing, and the combative character of the interactions between ethno-political organizations. The insistence on legal representation was created to "allow people's grievances to be more articulately presented on their behalf.[8] Fair hearing was very important to the Chairman and with a legal background he formulated the public sitting in a way similar to the legal space he was accustomed to."[9] The provision for petitioners to hire their own private lawyer if they could afford it created the situation where wealthier petitioners hired flamboyant lawyers who turned the public hearing into a courtroom by excessive use of legal jargon and cross examination. Rather than allowing for exposition of all accounts and details, they questioned petitioners solely to disprove the credibility of accounts presented. The following excerpt from the transcript of the public hearings is an example:

> Q: (Cross-examining lawyer): Now the figures you gave there state that there are estimated 6,000 Igbo civilians killed. It was not fact, it was just an estimate?
>
> A: (General Witness[10]): All other figures there are educated estimates.
>
> Q: Not facts?
>
> A: Facts when I say educated estimates.
>
> Q: No.
>
> A: Because we interviewed families.
>
> Q: Are these facts?
>
> A: Can I explain how we came at the figures?
>
> Q: No. Simple question, you said estimated 6,000 Igbo civilians and my question is simple, these are not facts, they are estimates?
>
> A: I said that I will not even answer that question. I said that they are educated estimates.
>
> Q: Thank you very much
>
> A: And if I explain to you why, you will find out why they are almost facts.
>
> Q: No, no, that is alright.[11]

Not only were there attempts to guide the telling of stories, the language with which the process was conducted was legalistic, as the following interaction suggests:

The Chairman of the Commission: Are we lawyers here? The thing is Exhibit 40 and you are telling me that it is not in evidence. I hope we are lawyers, let us talk as lawyers.

Chief Mogbo: As the Commission pleases, If my lord would grant me the indulgence-

The Chairman of the Commission: Chief Mogbo, do you have any objection to their withdrawing their witness for cross-examination and call him later so that we can make progress? If I am allowed, let him continue, if that would satisfy them. Have you any objection to that?

Chief Mogbo: My Lord, I still have a problem in understanding what their application is. The witness was put in the witness box by his counsel. The counsel got him to take the oath, after that, the witness was shown a document. The witness said, "I signed this document", and the Counsel says, "My Lord, I want to tender it" there was no objection and the document went in as Exhibit 40 before this Commission.

Such an atmosphere could not have presented a comfortable space for victims, unfamiliar with court procedures, to tell their stories. At different points, it would seem that the chairman noted and sought to defuse the legal atmosphere that prevailed but was unsuccessful:

Clerk: Petition no. 1648, Professor Nwabueze and others. Petitioners, I present my Lord.

Chairman: I do not need coming out, it is alright, if you are present. Appearances, please.

Mrs. Uwandu (Commission's lead counsel): May it please my Lord, honorable Commissioners, I announce my appearance for the Commission, I am Mrs. Chinwe Uwandu.

The Chairman: Yes.

Chief Umeadi: May it please my Lord, members of the Commission, I appear for the petitioners and the following are with me. Chief A.O. Mogbo SAN[12], Chief Enechi Onyia SAN, Senator Onyeabor SAN.[13]

In some instances the Chairman interrupted cross-examiners, especially when a direct victim was involved. For example, where a man who, at fifteen years old survived a mass shooting that killed his father and brothers because he was buried under falling bodies, was asked in cross-examination how he could remember the details he gave of the incident but could not remember the name of the soldier who commanded the killings over three decades ago, the Chairman subtly came to his defense.[14] However, it would seem that the lawyers could not distinguish between their usual court environment and the public space for truth and reconciliation. As seen below, the Chairman commented on this inability to separate the two:

> Mr. Gadzama: Thank you, he said that this is the response by Arewa Consultative Forum, my Lord I apply to tender it as an exhibit before this honorable Commission.
>
> Mr. Mogbo: My Lord and members, this matter had been flogged and my learned friend, my learned colleague should now be stopped from raising this issue or tendering or attempting to tender this document through a person who neither received it nor made it. He is not Ohaneze. Two, he did not make this document, so even if you had to cross examine him, it must be on a document which he made. There has been a ruling on this matter and I object to tendering it and secondly say that my learned friend should be stopped by the ruling earlier given on this matter.
>
> The Chairman: You people are converting this into a court of law. It is not a court of law.
>
> Mr. Gadzama: As the Commission pleases.[15]

Overall, these reminders did not change the image of the commission, confirming perceptions of the Commission as a quasi-public trial. Specific to the military and ethnic cases were affectations that included mode of entrance into the hearing space, that is, the ostentatious clothing, flashy cars, bodyguards adopted by the groups and their lawyers. The use of a team of high-ranking, often traditionally titled lawyers reaffirmed old class ideas of powerful legal representation where financial capabilities meant a team of lawyers rather than one lawyer. This showiness made more visible the politicization of the Commission by the ethno-political and military groups. Additionally, the Commission, whose reality as we argued in chapter one dictated a less retributive (trial approach), ended up with the trial procedure that Mertus criticized as "the dance of witness, lawyer and judge."[16] This adversarial, formal judicial format is inimical to the conception of justice as restorative, and more generally as practical, since the empirical goal of a truth commission is to lead a national conflict resolution process.

The final unintended outcome is the non-publication of a report that was promised to the public both by the Commission and the President. It is worth noting that Nigeria is not unique in this position. The Bolivian National Commission of Inquiry into Disappearances disbanded after three years of investigations without publishing a final report.[17] The Zimbabwean Commission of Inquiry established in 1985 was concluded, but its report was never published.[18] The Ugandan Commission of Inquiry into Violations of Human

Rights was established in 1986 but published its report in 1994 thereby giving it an unprecedented eight-year life span.[19] Therefore, the fate of the HRVIC report is not unusual.

The Nigerian president made promises to publish the report once it was presented to him. As stated by Mustapha, "In the course of his campaign for office, President Obasanjo promised to return Nigeria to its past glory . . . to return to the path of due process and the rule of law, and to eradicate the impunity enjoyed by erstwhile 'sacred cows'."[20] This led to the establishment of the HRVIC in the aftermath of his election. The president's statement at the inauguration of the HRVIC confirmed that the HRVIC was consistent with his government's "policy of openness and transparency in the conduct of government business."[21] His silence on the report now is a contradiction to this policy. In this, he is also not unique. The Alfonsin government in Argentina, which took a strong stand on human rights based on ethical convictions, had to modify its position under intense military pressure.[22] Therefore, subsequent and perhaps justifiable political pressures can affect the initial promises of a transitional government. Is this the case for Nigeria? It is may be possible that President Obasanjo, like President Alfosin, "staked out a position he could not sustain."[23] In the case of President Alfosin, he only had the legitimacy of a democratic election while the military elite "remained a cohesive force and maintained control over weapons."[24] President Obasanjo did not find himself in a similar position. While Nigeria's military leaders pose a potent threat to Obasanjo's government, he still remains one of them and is by virtue of his presidency the commander in chief of the armed forces. If anything, the military is more so divided in their loyalty to the different military personalities including Obasanjo, than they are a cohesive force against him.

The non–publication is much more plausibly explained by the fact that some of the high-ranking military officials who stand accused before the HRVIC are friends and fellow soldiers of the President. The highest-ranking controversial figure in the HRVIC process, the former military leader General Ibrahim Babangida was perceived by Nigerians to be "the only man who can frustrate Obasanjo's bid for re-election."[25] The argument follows that the non-publication of a report that in all probability indicts General Babangida is only a matter of political expediency. This argument weakens in Obasanjo's post re-election period, showing that General Babangida does not merely present a temporary political obstacle to the publication. He is not only the President's personal friend but has served as his presidential representative as stated earlier. Therefore, the non-publication of the report is partly an indication of President Obasanjo's personal predicament of being conflicted between loyalty to friends who propelled him into his presidency and loyalty and duty to the country as the President. It may also partly indicate that the popularity of the Commission and some of its unintended outcomes were not expected by the Obasanjo government who now wish for the HRVIC to disappear.

Furthermore, the decisions of the Commission on the Obasanjo case are bound to be controversial regardless of its stance and therefore may be implicated in the non-publication of the report. A positive judgment by the Commission is bound to attract the criticism of the public and might consequently diminish the credibility of the Commission's final report as well as the government's credibility. On the other hand, holding the President culpable of accusations leveled against him, with similar decisions on fellow military friends, will very likely cause the President to withhold the report.

The lack of public pressure for the publication of the report before the re-election period might also seem to the president a sign of the public's indifference to the report. Thus, the publication of the report will not confer political advantage since there is more elite pressure to withhold the report than public pressure to publish it. In this light, Obasanjo's government may not be a transitional government, after all. As stated in chapter one, democracies can be unjust governments as the politics of silence and lack of transparency and accountability are telltale signs of an unjust government.

As stated by one of the commissioners, who was disappointed with what he deemed the government's lack of integrity and the public's lack of civic responsibility, "the truth of the matter is that the Nigerian political system is intensely hostile to certain principles we all aspire to. We all know what we like but the process of getting from point A to B is what we don't want to commit ourselves to."[26] Whether such sentiments will compel the commissioners to publish the report without the approval of the government is unknown. All commissioners presently assert that they will not publish the report without the government's permission. This stance is, however, vulnerable to time and circumstances.

This raises the issue about the moral and political obligations of the Commission in the face of the non-publication of the report. As Nduka-Eze states,

> The publication of the report will be in the public's interest because, foremost, it says to the Nigerian people, that the Commission serves them first. Secondly because it allows for the people to have an idea of their recommendations and can allow non–state groups to start implementing things that need not be implemented by the state. The ultimate goal here is to heal our nation. The government is not going to do everything and it will be good to make the people aware of their role in reconciling the nation.[27]

It could be argued that without a parliamentary act, the Commission, as an establishment of the President, is not subject to the people and cannot legally publish the report if pressured by the public. It can also be argued that moral obligations as well as civic duty compels them to put the needs of the country before the whims of the executive arm of the government. They could bring the report for ratification before the parliament as the democratic and enduring representative body of the people leading to another possible unintended development of the HRVIC process.

Given the realities that the HRVIC contended with in the pursuit of its ideals of truth and reconciliation, and the resulting non-publication of the report, can it be said that it made no contribution whatsoever to Nigeria's transitional process? To what the extent the HRVIC had an impact on the Nigerian polity and the lessons to be learned from it is the subject of the next and concluding chapter.

NOTES

1. See Shea (1999).
2. See Shea (1999).
3. Barrister Nduka-Eze, Counsel for the Asaba People, interview by author, Lagos Nigeria, September 25, 2003.
4. *Today*, 9–15 January 2000.
5. By time of publishing this book, the injunction case had been resolved, but not after approximately two years after the Commission handed its report to the government.
6. For Stella Obasanjo's presence on behalf of her husband at Babangida's daughter's wedding, see "Aisha Babangida's Wedding," *Vanguard*, September 10, 2003, Paper Copy. General Ibrahim Babangida, a non-state official, represented the Nigerian government in state talks with Zambian and Sudanese Presidents. See *West Africa*, December 13–19, 1999.
7. *Today*, January 8, 2000.
8. Mrs. Chinwe Uwandu, Lead Counsel for the Human Rights Violations Investigation Commission., interview by author, New Haven, Connecticut, August 26, 2003.
9. Uwandu, interview.
10. General witnesses were particular to ethno-political organizations who had one member of the organization witness to all the events detailed in the petition. The general witness account was supplemented with accounts from eyewitnesses or victims to affirm specific events within the petition.
11. Verbatim Report 2002, 81–91.
12. Senior Advocate of Nigeria is the highest honorable title that a lawyer can be called to in Nigeria in recognition of legal excellence.
13. Verbatim Report 2002, 2.
14. Verbatim Report 2002, 73–75.

15. Verbatim Report 2002, 104.

16. Julie Mertus, "Truth in a Box: The Limits of Justice through Judicial Mechanisms," in *The Politics of Memory: Truth, Healing and Social Justice*, ed. Ifi Amadiume and Abdullahi An-Na'im (London and New York: Zed Books 2000), 142.

17. Priscilla B. Hayner, "Fifteen Truth Commissions–1974 to 1994: A Comparative Study," *Human Rights Quarterly* 16, No. 4 (1994).

18. Priscilla B. Hayner, "Fifteen Truth Commissions."

19. Priscilla B. Hayner, "Fifteen Truth Commissions."

20. Raufu A. Mustapha, "*Ethnicity and the Politics of Democratization in Nigeria: Structure, Transformations and Processes*" (paper for a Workshop on Ethnicity and Democracy in Africa, Queen's University, Kingston, Ontario, Canada, March 2000), 6.

21. *Vanguard*, February 13, 2004, paper copy.

22. Jose Zalaquett, "Balancing Ethical Imperatives and Political Constraints: The Dilemma of New Democracies Confronting Past Human Rights Violations," *43 Hastings Law Journal* 1425 9 (1991–1992); See also Carlos Nino, "The Duty to Punish Past Abuses put into Context: The Case for Argentina," *100 Yale Law Journal 26199* (1991).

23. Jose Zalaquett, "Balancing Ethical Imperatives and Political Constraints," 43.

24. Jose Zalaquett, "Balancing Ethical Imperatives and Political Constraints," 43.

25. "Dele Giwa: Between Law and Politics," *ThisDayonline*, July 9, 2002 <http://www.thisdayonline.com/archive/2002/07/09/20020709law09.html>, Accessed January 3, 2004.

26. Father Matthew Kukah, Member of the Human Rights Violations Investigation Commission, interview by author, Cambridge, Mass., August 15, 2003.

27. Nduka-Eze, interview.

Chapter Five

Conclusion: Situating the HRVIC

INTRODUCTION

According to Villa-Vicencio and Verwoerd, the TRC was not aimed at reconciling South Africans with one another, as such a goal would not have been achievable. Rather it was set up to contribute toward laying the foundation on which national unity and reconciliation could be built.[1] In like manner, the two-year term of the HRVIC was not aimed at the instant dislodging of long-standing means of political engagement such as ethnic conflict or military violence. It could only help to consolidate a nascent democracy by sketching, through its sittings and final report, "the road map that can transform Nigeria into a united and democratic society where the rule of law is upheld and human rights are respected."[2] That seemed to be the expectation of the Nigerian public, as reflected in the press. This gave rise to renewed public interest in a government that had been criticized as a democratic cloak for further military rule and evoked new reflections on a past which now seemed truly dislocated from the present with the establishment of the HRVIC. Thus, the HRVIC was intended to provide the process for that formal reinsertion of the past into the present, in order to re-signify it through the vista of the public's aspirations for the nation's future. Though Nigeria's form of practical justice was not well defined, hindsight indicates that this re-signification was a vital part of it.

HRVIC AND MEMORY MAKING

The HRVIC succeeded in providing a formal space for re-signifying the past through a prism of future hopes. Despite the antagonistic note of the petitions, ethnic organizations couched their petition in the notion of reconciliation, thus acknowledging that the current condition of social relations was inimical to a better Nigeria. However, with the absence of a clearly defined format of presentation, the re-signification of historical memory was guided by particular perspectives that operated within the wider framework of the petitioners' disposition to the HRVIC. The formal space was appropriated by the most politically visible section of the public, the ethno-political elite, who used the space for the re-signification of the past through the vista of sectarian political objectives. Thus, the achievement of the group's particular expectations was seen as the conduit to a better Nigeria. J. R. Gillis in *Memory and Identity* terms this re-signification of the past, memory-work, and argues that it is like "any other kind of physical or mental labor, embedded in complex class, gender and power relations that determine *what is remembered (or forgotten), by whom and for what end*."[3] Through memory work, events and actions are re-signified. This re-signification is termed by Norval as 'aspect change.'[4] For Norval, the South African TRC achieved this by providing the context in which lost or hidden histories were recovered or unearthed, and identities and memories were renegotiated "through the documentation and public exposure of gross human rights violations."[5]

REFRAMING HISTORY

The application of Norval's 'aspect change' theory to the Ohaneze petition exposes the appropriation of Biafra for the case of Igbo marginalization, even though, as Amadiume argues, the "discourses on Biafra go beyond the claims of Igbo marginalization."[6] The objectives of the group regarding the HRVIC centered on marginalization and the Biafra stories were told within that context. For example, as shown in chapter three, the pogroms came before the Commission as evidence for marginalization efforts against the Igbos in the wake of the January coup and not as discrete direct cases of human rights violation.

Selective accounting of events and silence regarding the complicity of those at the helm of these warring ethno-political organizations indicated the ways in which the mandate to 'tell the truth' was interpreted and reformulated as the mandate to 'tell *our* story.' Relative to the other truth commissions that guided the HRVIC process, the telling of 'our story' in Nigeria's truth commission took a different approach in the case of petitions from sectarian groups. Ethno-political groups submitted collective petitions that situated individual accounts as affirmations of the group's collective story. They ensured the containment of individual stories within the boundaries of the collective story. The Ohaneze petition presented "witnesses" to the longstanding violation of the human rights of Igbo persons in the north through insurgencies and the misconduct of the Nigerian government during the civil war. However, there were none to tell the stories of the misconduct of the Biafran government during the war, such as the summary execution of suspected 'saboteurs,'[7] thus maintaining a particular perspective of the collective story. Individuals told the stories of their victimization as 'witnesses' to a collective petition that addressed the victimization of Igbos as a collective body. This process of memory-making entailed the attribution of guilt to a collective 'other.' One respondent, on being asked if there were empathetic northerners who hid and/or saved the lives of easterners during the 1966 pogroms, first refused to answer but eventually and reluctantly said, "Yes. But that was the exception and we did it too. My family helped Hausa people when they [easterners] were expelling the Hausas."[8]

In contrast to this attitude is the story of a Tutsi woman in Rwanda who showed the complexity of culpability in violent pasts and the need for individual rather than collective culpability regarding ethnic conflicts. She stated, "they [Hutu family] hid me in their house and gave me somewhere to sleep. My two children survived also. I hid them deep inside a hole. I gave them food at night given to me by the Hutu whose house I was staying at . . . They can hide you but after, go out and kill others."[9] Such an account presents the more realistic nature of human relationships that transcend ethnic identity and boundary. A personal relationship in this instance suppressed political antagonism to the particular individual but did not necessarily eliminate the antagonism all together. However, the Nigerian ethno-political groups, having strategized a position, could not allow for such diverging accounts within their petition. In ensuring intra-group consensus, these groups consequently prevented inter-group consensus and a nuanced perspective of the past.

This notion of the continuing reformation of identity is not a novel idea. As Bardhan argued:

> The ideology of identity is, of course, socially constructed, as historical memories are adapted and traditions are often invented. There is a certain fluidity and malleability in the boundaries of community identity or in the mythology of ethnicity-based nationalities or sub-nationalities as 'imagined communities.' That gives considerable leverage to political leaders bent on using ethnicity as a mobilization device. As Ignatieff (1993) comments, "it is not how the past dictates to the present but how the present manipulates the past that is decisive."[10]

Memory work in the HRVIC, for these ethno-political groups, became a process of formalizing patterns of identity (re) making for the procurement of what was perceived to be due them from the national sphere, not only in terms of resources for the group but also in terms of external perception of the group.

EVALUATING THE HRVIC

Reconciliation

Even if they are criticized for their inability to deliver certain forms of justice, truth commissions are noted by most writers for their recognition and restoration of the human and civil dignity of victims.[11] Only through such recognition is reconciliation possible.[12] Norval argues that it is important for attempts at reconciliation to take place in public. The HRVIC contributed to the formation of a shared public space where different voices were heard and perhaps a common memory was created. The extent of that common memory is an important measure of how unified the country is, since it is not only what is remembered but also how the society interacts with memories that determines collective identity.[13] Without the published final report, all that has been achieved in Nigeria is the wider dissemination of long-held but revitalized beliefs. As highlighted in chapter four, many groups found problems with the final report of the South African TRC and consequently publicly denounced it.[14] Yet, President Mandela accepted it as the formal collective memory of the nation. President Obasanjo neither released the report as the collective memory of the Nigerian people, of nor did he apologize to victims on behalf of past perpetrator governments, in like manner to President Patricio Aylwin of Chile on his presentation of the report to the public. If the institution of a collective memory or some official acknowledgment of the victimization is a prerequisite to reconciliation of any sort, the process seems then to have been aborted in Nigeria.

On the other hand, the publication of a final report does not guarantee the report being viewed as a collective memory rather than perhaps a 'compromised' consensus and set of recommendations arrived at within the context of a negotiated transition.[15] As such, in a deeply divided society, publication or non-publication of a report might prove nugatory to the reconciliation process. The attitude of the state and civil society, now armed with information, towards the containment of conflict might be deemed more important and relevant.

Truth

Most aspects of truth commissions, including their very terms of reference, are inevitably engaged with politics. Truth commissions work with full knowledge and acceptance that truths are contextualized in what Norval defines as, "wider frames of reference," the political context of memory-making.[16] For Norval, the idea that gaining knowledge of the past through truth-telling, that is, asking what really happened, will lead to a change in attitude is misleading. Change is brought about by aspect change: a shift in the way in which things are perceived rather than by appeal to reality as if it is unmediated.[17] The HRVIC provides the possibility, but only a possibility, for this aspect change. Furthermore, Asmal, Asmal, and Roberts argue that the South African TRC was only one means of dismantling the old monolithic structure of truth to replace it with a multiplicity of narratives. The [TRC] does not possess a monopoly on the mechanism for "historical rectification."[18] The non-publication of the Nigerian HRVIC report may have unwittingly produced a multiplicity of narratives for the Nigerian people about their past, since the nation heard, within a common space, different perspectives of history, especially those perspectives that they were not usually privy to.

Justice

The argument for the absence of a monopolistic nature in the South African TRC is contestable, given that its provision of amnesty effectively denied citizens of other equally valid, legal and socially acceptable means of seeking 'historical rectification'. This is not the case in Nigeria where prosecution, as in the Argentine case, is feasible, and given the existence of a possibly damning report, likely under a reformed Nigerian legal system. Yet out of the Guatemalan, Ugandan, South African, Chilean, and Argentine cases that guided the HRVIC, only the Argentine government prosecuted perpetrators. In fact, the Argentine prosecutions ceased in the face of political pressure. For similar reasons, Nigeria will likely conform to the majority.

Without prosecutions as in the Argentine case, how can the impact of the HRVIC be evaluated? Can the outcome or effects of truth commissions be realistically measured? Perhaps, interviews of victims/petitioners in the post-hearings period can show the extent to which that basic process was helpful or not to them. Rating the occurrence of ethnic insurgencies in the post-HRVIC era may also serve as a measuring stick for the success of HRVIC is in initiating the reconciliation process with respect to the Arewa and Ohaneze petitions. An investigation could be carried out into the extent to which the government institutionalized recommended responses to grievances within a specified time period. A further, more quantitative investigation could take a cross-sectional survey of ethnic opinions of the 'other' and the 'self' in the post-HRVIC period. Such activities should be the responsibility of academics of truth commissions and human rights organizations in order to inform other states with high ethnic discord about the viability of truth commissions as a way of dealing with the past in their transitional period.

Even if it is difficult to measure the effectiveness of truth commissions in dealing with problems of identity and trauma in transitional societies, it is much more difficult to judge their ability to render justice. It can be argued that the airing of accounts within a formal public space and the provision of a voice for victims allow for the beginning of the first form of reconciliation, that is, the individual reconciliation to long bottled up traumatic events of the past. As noted earlier, this inevitably renders Fraser's recognitive form of justice, even if it may seem paltry. Yet, there is much room to argue that recognitive justice was not the strongest form of practical justice that Nigeria could have delivered. Again, an official report that would be read to the Nigerian public and widely disseminated could inspire the enactment of justice measures at both the government and organizational levels, that is, measures that might rearrange the social relations in Nigeria.

As argued in chapter one, the justice of truth commissions is practical. It is spatially and temporally defined to respond to the pragmatic needs of a transitional society, making what is sufficient justice for an individual or a group not necessarily the case for others. Justice for the different ethnicities would differ in an attempt to bring them to a place of equality. Without a report, there is no indication of which conceptions of justice within the practical justice spectrum the HRVIC process will engender. Perhaps it will be capped at the sort of recognitive justice that it has served or expand to restorative forms of justice and beyond. Time will tell. Thus, it is even much more difficult to measure its impact. Landsman suggests that even if we cannot calculate the effectiveness of truth commissions, we can at least reject such an approach to dealing with the past in the circumstances where,

> The commission is not structured to make a thorough inquiry or exacerbates delay; compensation is not paid to victims; the commission is not a product of democratic decision-making; the commission does not yield at least four to six benefits of prosecution;[19] exigent social, economic, or political factors make more complete compliance impossible.[20]

In this way, objectives are assessed before a truth commission is established in order to control, as much as possible, its outcome. By doing so, a truth commission is made more precise by ensuring that it first meets certain criteria for delivering measurable justice for the particular socio-political context that necessitated it. Landsman calls for a high threshold for a truth commission. The notion of a thorough inquiry can be an area of contestation. The HRVIC dealt with 200 cases as opposed to the 2,920 cases dealt with by the Chilean Commission. The measures that may be used to determine a thorough inquiry in each case will differ. In some instances, victims may not be looking for compensation but acknowledgment. As argued in chapter one, a truth commission as part of practical justice, in so far as the truth telling stage is concerned, is the starting point of justice. Therefore, it cannot be required to yield the prosecution benefits that Landsman refers to. Truth commissions should be understood to prepare the ground of possibilities with respect to justice. Measuring the HRVIC against Landsman's criteria, it may fail to meet the standard required to establish a truth commission. However, as a starting point of practical justice that entails the potential for restorative, distributive, reparative, and even retributive justice, the HRVIC has served its purpose. The responsibility for the realization of its possibilities now lies with the government and the Nigerian people.

CONCLUSION

The idea of a truth commission legitimized on such contested concepts as justice and truth means that there are no easy answers to the questions it poses. According to Tina Rosenberg in Meredith's *Coming to Terms*, "when Apartheid finally gave way to full democracy in 1994, South Africa invested most of its hope for dealing with its past in one institution: the Truth and Reconciliation Commission."[21] Can the same be said for Nigeria? To a great degree, the Nigerian people, if not the government, despite the initial skepticism came to see the HRVIC as *the hope* for dealing with Nigerian's violent past. However, how the HRVIC process embedded itself within the Nigerian reality is the curious matter which will require more time to reveal itself.

Chapter one concluded that truth commissions are generally established to investigate human rights abuses and recommend the procedures to guide the prevention of their recurrence and are pragmatic solutions to problematic transitions. They arise out of the "muck of forced compromises" made by a new era government that is vulnerable to the old order.[22] More importantly, they respond to the practical needs of a negotiated transition, making it an ideal justice mechanism for the transitional circumstances for which they are appropriate. Practical justice, couched as a spectrum of the different conceptions of justice, is then what Rawls argues to be 'political,' "an agreed basis for public justification in matters of justice."[23] Truth as the starting point of justice is the potential consensus that a commission seeks to find in politicized accounts of the past. Justice in this light is primarily concerned the creation or preservation of equality in social relations. Here, a truth commission, having been determined to be appropriate for Nigeria's situation, allows us to examine the nature of Nigeria's transition within the contested discourses of justice, reconciliation, truth, and the politicization of memory.

The nature of Nigeria's new democracy is elaborated in chapter two through the presentation of the context within which the HRVIC was established and the realities that faced such an 'ideal' mechanism for coming to terms with the past. The inevitable politicization of the HRVIC, given its domestic control and lack of thorough pre-setup preparation, runs through the account of the HRVIC process. This reality confirms the argument in chapter one that truth commissions are not only defined by intentions but also actions, not only by ideals and convictions but also by practicality, not only by moral but also political considerations. This makes the actions, for example, the public hearings and the invitation to civil society organizations, to take part in brainstorming sessions about the proposed role of the HRVIC, part of rendering practical justice.

Chapter three, which dealt with key ethnic petitions before the HRVIC, highlighted two important and related lessons. The first is that the HRVIC cannot engage with Nigeria's past outside the context of ethnic politics. Different modes of political engagement have through the years been ethnicized. The Ohaneze versus Arewa petition made the case that the perpetual state of mutual ethnic animosity is sometimes deliberate. Mustapha, paraphrasing Bardhan, asserts that "behind the madness of every ethnic conflict lies not really visceral antagonism but a political and economic logic of exclusion and competition over limited resources. The *recourse to histories of past antagonism often serves as a legitimating factor*." [24] The extensive nature of Nigeria's ethnic politics distinguishes it from the South African, Chilean, and Argentine cases from which the HRVIC sought ideas. In Nigeria, 'marginalization' or repression was framed within the discourse of cultural, if not ethnic, identity that was confirmed by historical narratives of sustained repression. The ethnic petitions represented grievances that were full of apologetics and empty of apologies for their role in the violence of the past. They, therefore, ignored questions of responsibility, moral or otherwise, that arose out of such histories.

The second is that due to the manner in which the HRVIC arose, and given the deliberate shaping of grievances, petitioners were not unrealistic in their expectations from the HRVIC process. For some of the victims within the Ohaneze petition, the HRVIC was used to legitimize individual stories and thus recognitive justice was served for such individuals. For the collective, the compilation of grievances was part of the process of consolidating 'a history' for posterity and, for securing political, economic, and social resources for the present. As such, the HRVIC may have been appropriated without its consent. Could it have prevented its use in this manner or was that, in fact, part of its role?

Chapter four dealt with this question by exploring the unintended developments that were engendered by the existence of the HRVIC. The form of inquiry was itself important. The public hearings, by using legal language and procedures, confirmed the HRVIC as a quasi-judicial process in order to provide a certain validation to its outcome. Consequently, the HRVIC, perhaps unwittingly, validated a formal space for memory-making and the long-standing practice of politicizing memory.

The visibility of what became the contradictory nature of the HRVIC is indicated in two key examples. The first is the questioning of the new era president, the originator of the HRVIC, as a perpetrator of human rights abuses. The second is the eventual adoption of the cross-examination tactic of a court procedure for the sake of fair hearing and 'zeroing' in on the truth. The public hearing that aimed at providing a safe space for victims was to end up as an arena for victims' prosecuting lawyers and the defense lawyers of the accused to exhibit their legal panache through tricky cross-examination of 'witnesses', that is, real or perceived victims. It is not surprising that the HRVIC, in using such adversarial methods in its proceedings, hosted rather than stemmed ethnic tensions. To what degree this approach affected victims in the post-hearing period is unknown. However, such an approach can only negatively affect the potential for reconciliation.

Generally, truth commissions and studies of them have generated more questions than answers. The HRVIC process is not an exception. This is due to the socio-political nature of the process. As Gallie argued we can only arrive at unanimous answers when "our chief concern is with the use or manifestation of reason in science; but it fails completely as a description of those elements of reason that make possible discussions of religious, political, and artistic problems."[25]

Whether or not the HRVIC has achieved any of it goals, at each stage, it has produced supporters and dissenters guided by distinct interests. The truth commission and its effects can be argued to have been fleeting or firmly grounded, depending on the perspective adopted. The questions that arise from its presence, however viewed, are nonetheless important. Given that the negotiated nature of Nigeria's transition called for a truth commission, was its form the right form for Nigeria? With a narrower time frame, perhaps according to the first mandate, which excluded the civil war era, would the nature of the HRVIC's engagement with the question of ethnicity have been different? Without an official report, what impact has it made? What lessons can be learned in hindsight?

Ultimately, it is not possible to reach any final conclusive and definitive judgment regarding the achievements and failures of the work of the HRVIC. This is the case for many reasons but most importantly, due to the contemporary nature of its work. The potential for the re-engagement of civil society with the HRVIC work is still viable. For example, civil society organizations continue to agitate for the official publication of the report. As such, its overall success or failure can only be fully ascertained with the passage of time.

Yet, some conclusions can be drawn about the HRVIC. The Nigerian public was privileged to hear not only the voices they were accustomed to hearing but also the other voices legitimated by the Commission. The sight of the Nigerian president as a participant before the HRVIC must have impacted the Nigerian audience, given their experience with past dictators who commanded "above the law" status. Also, the military connections of the government that produced the HRVIC and the predominance of ethnic politics in the country, both of which were not factored into the development of the HRVIC, affected its engagement with Nigerian citizens. In retrospect, it is obvious that the business of cutting and pasting from the South African experience was bound to fail, for the reason that the historical factors that gave rise to the TRC were unique to South Africa. The unique depths of ethnic tension and military involvement in Nigeria required a careful conceptualization of how a truth commission might work, that did not try to mimic Chile, Argentina, or South Africa but, which took cognizance of the socio-political factors unique to Nigeria. Questions of justice, truth, and reconciliation should have been interpreted through the framework of Nigeria's own particular reality as one model of a truth commission for a heterogeneous continent is naıve. These are guiding lessons particularly for, countries with histories of ethnic strife which may want to engage in this form of transitional justice.

Furthermore, as seen in chapter one, justice and truth are concepts that are not definitive. In the negotiated political situation that engenders truth commissions, justice becomes what is realistically achievable. While prosecutions as retributive justice might remain the Thrasymachian "advantage of the stronger" (Plato, *The Republic*), truth commissions as part of restorative justice tend to enforce a recognition of the weaker and prepare for the reestablishment of equality between the two. Truth is exposed as re-historicization, made at the dawn of a society's new era in an effort to position such an era within the society's entire history. Reconciliation, as argued by Christie, is defined and prescribed according to the perspectives from which varied groups interpret their memories. It can be ethical, religious, political, or economic[26] and these varied interpretations make reconciliation a contested and difficult goal. Truth Commissions examined through these interpretations of justice, truth and reconciliation become not only a process for dealing with the past but the actual and immediate reflection of the discord and confusion that is the legacy of the past and the inheritance of the new era government. The discourse of discontinuity in fact becomes one of continuity, and such a scenario captures the practical state of the Nigerian truth commission, its process, and the non-publication of its official report.

NOTES

1. Charles Villa-Vicencio, "Getting on with Life: A Move towards Reconciliation," in *Looking Back Reaching Forward, Reflections on the Truth and Reconciliation Commission of South Africa*, ed. Charles Villa-Vicencio and Wilhelm Verwoerd (Cape Town: University of Cape Town Press, 2000), 199.
2. *Vanguard*, February 13, 2004, paper copy.
3. Cited in Aletta Norval, "Truth and Reconciliation: The Birth of the Present and the Reworking of History," *Journal of Southern African Studies* 25 (1999): 499–519, (my emphasis).
4. Norval, "Truth and Reconciliation."
5. Norval, "Truth and Reconciliation," 500.
6. Ifi Amadiume, "Biafra and Intellectual Responsibility," in *The Politics of Memory: Truth, Healing and Social Justice*, ed. Ifi Amadiume and Abdullahi An-Na'im (London and New York: Zed Books 2000).
7. Nneoma V. Nwogu, "Ethnic Revivalism: Recasting the Legacy of the Nigerian Civil War" (BA Thesis, Wellesley College, 2002).
8. Chief Eze-Ozogbu, Chairman of Ohaneze Ndi Igbo, interview by author, Enugu, Nigeria, September 9, 2003.
9. Jason Pronyk, "N*egotiating the Past': An Examination of the Methods Chosen by Rwanda and South Africa for Dealing with Justice*," (MPhil Thesis in Development Studies. International Development Center, Queen Elizabeth House, University of Oxford, 2000), 106.
10. Pranab Bardhan, "*Method in the Madness? A Political Economy Analysis of Ethnic Conflicts in Less Developed Countries,*' Center for International and Development Economics Research. Working Paper No. C96-070, University of California, Berkeley, 1996, 14–15.
11. For sources, see Landsman (1996), Kritz (1996), Tutu (1999), Meredith (1999), Rothberg and Thompson (2000), Villa-Vicencio and Verwoerd (2000), Graybill (2002).
12. Elizabeth Kiss, "Moral Ambition Within and Beyond Political Constraints: Reflections on Restorative Justice," in *Truth V. Justice*, ed. Robert Rotberg and Dennis Thompson (Princeton, NJ: Princeton University Press, 2000).
13. Niebhur, quoted in Norval, "Truth and Reconciliation," 513.
14. See Dorothy Shea, "Are TCs Just A Fad? Indicators and Implications for South Africa" (paper presented at University of Witswatersrand June 11–19, 1999 Conference: TRC Commissioning the Past, 1999).
15. Mahmood Mamdani, "Truth According to the TRC," in *The Politics of Memory: Truth, Healing and Social Justice*, ed. Ifi Amadiume and Abdullahi An-Na'im (London and New York: Zed Books, 2000).
16. Norval, "Truth and Reconciliation."
17. Norval, "Truth and Reconciliation."
18. Asmal K., Asmal L., and Roberts R, *Reconciliation through Truth: A Reckoning of Apartheid's Criminal Governance*, 2nd Edition (Oxford: James Currey, 1997), 214.

19. Landsman lists the six benefits of prosecution, which are as follows: enhancement of the prospects for the establishment of the rule of law, a means of educating the citizenry as to the nature and extent of prior wrongdoing, a means of identifying and creating the standard for the compensation of victims, a means of punishing perpetrators, a means to enhance a society's ability to deter future violations and to serve as an essential means of healing social wounds caused by serious human rights violations. Stephen Landsman, "Accountability for International Crime and Serious Violations of Fundamental Human Rights: Alternative Responses to Serious Human Rights Abuses: Of Prosecution and Truth Commissions," *59 Law and Contemporary Problems* 81 (1996).

20. See Stephen Landsman, "Accountability for International Crime and Serious Violations of Fundamental Human Rights."

21. Martin Meredith, *Coming to Terms, South Africa's Search for Truth* (New York: Public Affairs, 1999), x.

22. See Lawrence Weschler, *A Miracle, A Universe: Settling Accounts with Torturers* (New York: Pantheon, 1990).

23. John Rawls, *Political Liberalism* (New York: Columbia University Press, 1993), 150–51.

24. Bardhan (1996), cited in Raufu A. Mustapha, "*Ethnicity and the Politics of Democratization in Nigeria: Structure, Transformations and Processes*" (paper for a Workshop on Ethnicity and Democracy in Africa, Queen's University, Kingston, Ontario, Canada, March 2000), my emphasis.

25. Walter B.Gallie, "Essentially Contested Concepts," *Proceedings of the Aristotelian Society* 56, (1955–56), 196.

26. Kenneth Christie, *The South African Truth Commission* (New York: St Martin's Press, 2000).

Afterword[1]

In the Foreword to the HRVIC Report, Justice Chukwudifu Oputa, the Chairman of the Commission begins by identifying the Report as a lament.[2] Reading like poetic verses, the first few paragraphs speak directly to Nigerian citizens, chronicling the source of what he calls the "aftermath of military rule and the consequential disappearance, violations of the human rights and essential freedoms of Nigerians. . . . [and] the decay of our society."[3] Citing the return to democratic rule on May 29, 1999, he states that there is now a chance for a better society, "the opportunity for us to rise above this decay, to break the silence of the past and to forge ahead, determined to lay to rest the ghost of this dark and painful period in our national history."[4]

The Report, which begins with this note of lamentation, reconciliation, and healing seeks (and achieves) the encapsulation of Nigeria's dream for a stable and rights-conscious society. It meticulously goes through different institutions in Nigeria to highlight ways of restructuring the institutional framework to prevent rights violations and strengthen the observance of rights. In this way, it lays the groundwork for a generative form of justice, that is, one that does not reinstate what was in place but creates something new out of the lessons of the past. This approach still remains restorative in so far as it seeks to restore the equality in the different relations within society and it is practical because it takes into consideration the lessons of the past in the context of what is achievable for the country. The report names perpetrators such as the generals but does not name any names that were not already in the public sphere. The HRVIC's public condemnation and presentation for possible prosecution of the generals is punitive in nature thus borrowing from retributive justice. The report recommends that the President apologize to the nation on behalf of the state. Thus, it opens the forum for the state to recognize and acknowledge its guilt and, at the same time, acknowledge the victimization of those who suffered both directly at the hands of the state and indirectly by the omissions of the state in protecting its citizens. The report recommends both dignitary and monetary reparation. As such the HRVIC sought to turn the Nigerian state into a nation.[5] The recommendations were particularly exhaustive, couched in a grand and noble idea of a new Nigeria as though a re-declaration of independence. As such, the HRVIC's work corresponds to the notion of practical justice that used the context of Nigerian history and state of transition to guide the mix of the different conceptions of justice that it deemed appropriate for Nigeria.

Dealing with the particular issues raised in this book, the HRVIC's recommendation was consistent with the argument raised in chapter two that practical justice allows the HRVIC to recommend prosecution for the generals who ignored their summons since by virtue of their refusal to participate, they chose the isolating path of retributive justice over reintegration into society. The Report recommended the reopening of cases implicating the generals for investigation and possible prosecution.[6]

However, the HRVIC was silent on the Kuti Family petition[7] implicating the President for violation of human rights during his military rule. While the record of the hearings shows that the case had been litigated in courts as well as dealt with through a different inquiry, it remains curious that the HRVIC did not mention the case in its recommendations even if it were to claim judicial deference. There were many commissions of inquiry under different military regimes and if the HRVIC investigated violations relating those issues such as the Abandoned Property issues raised by Ohaneze, it would be in a weak position to argue that the issue had already been adjudicated properly.

As suspected, the HRVIC was also silent on the issue of the pogroms focusing, as shown, in chapter three on the issue of marginalization. The HRVIC found that marginalization while a contested notion, was a common complaint among the different ethno-political petitions. The Commission determined marginalization to signify the groups' "fears of the curtailment or violation of [their] substantive human rights."[8] Consequently, the HRVIC recommended "the political restructuring of our federal system of government, underlined by equitable and fair resource allocation and distribution" as the solution to marginalization.[9] Beyond that, they sought to reformulate the identity of Nigerians from one of sectarian affiliation to a national identity. It harkens to an old anthem which recognizes diversity but prioritizes unity. It quotes "though tribes and tongues may differ, in brotherhood we stand . . . Nigerians all."[10] The Commission as a official historical accounting of the nation's history also dealt with the dissension surrounding the January 15 coup by acknowledging the good motivations of the first coup but affirmed it as the beginning of a destructive practice that unfolded in the country.

In many ways, the Commission circumvented any hard rulings on particularly volatile petitions like Ohaneze and Arewa's and sought more to bring about structural changes in the country that could diffuse the marginalization that they viewed as the underlying harm. As such the Commission was clearly cognizant of the need to repair a broken social relationship between different societal cleavages. It states,

> there were genuine concerns among the petitioners and the generality of our people, the citizens, that Nigerians need a nation to belong to, a nation cemented by a social contract of mutuality and reciprocity in cultural, economic, political and social relations, a nation to be proud of, one that provides its citizens with an enabling umbrella of equality of opportunities, social and distributive justice, protection and security. From the sentiments re-echoed in messages received and the keen interest demonstrated in the mandate and work of the Commission by innumerable Nigerians, within and outside our country, we are convinced that, with the right social, economic and political atmosphere, a united, powerful, purposeful, compassionate and egalitarian nation will emerge from the frustrations expressed and captured by such expressions as *marginalization, stranger, indigene, discrimination,* etc.[11]

In conclusion, it seems that those who were skeptical of President Obasanjo's motives may now be vindicated given that the government has not officially released the report. Indeed the report and its recommendations, as prophesied in 2000 by a columnist, has ended up on government "shelves gathering dust."[12] Furthermore, President Obasanjo, who welcomed the presentation of the report, has since not publicly spoken on it nor has he apologized as was recommended by the report on behalf of the state. This is similar to the Sierra Leonean case where President Kabbah refused to apologize to the Sierra Leonean people on behalf of the state as recommended by the Sierra Leonean Truth Commission.[13] It is difficult to understand why a President of a new eras government who sets up or supports a truth commission and even participates in its processes would choose to ignore the results of the Commission's efforts. As earlier noted, it is apparent that the HRVIC has laid down the potential for more than it has currently achieved. To deny those possibilities to the society, victims and perpetrators in particular, who have awakened memories in an effort to help the country move forward, would impose a new set of injustice.

Finally, the work of civil society organizations cannot suffice with respect to the tasks that remain unfinished with the HRVIC process. They cannot give the report the sort of legitimacy it requires from the government nor can they implement any significant portion of the institutional restructuring on which the HRVIC grounds the new social arrangement for a rights-conscious Nigeria. In that light, the work of civil society organizations must focus on popularizing the cause of the HRVIC report so as to engender a political response from Nigerians. Constituencies that demand that their representatives be accountable vis-à-vis the HRVIC recommendations will also provide the fertile ground in which the report and recommendation, when legitimized by the government, can take effect.

NOTES

1. Two civil society organizations, named the Nigerian Democratic Movement and the Nigerian Civil Society Forum were the first organizations to publish and circulate the HRVIC report in 2005 after the original manuscript for this book was completed. As such, I had access to the report only after the completion of the manuscript and added this Afterword in light of the report. While the publication does not materially alter the contents of the preceding chapters, access to the report has helped clarify some speculations and answer questions posed in those chapters and they are explored in this section.
2. Synoptic Overview of the HRVIC Report: Conclusions and Recommendations including Chairman's Foreword, May 2002, Foreword, paragraph 1.1.
3. Synoptic Overview of the HRVIC Report, Foreword, paragraph 1.1–1.3.
4. Synoptic Overview of the HRVIC Report, Foreword, paragraph 1.5.
5. Synoptic Overview of the HRVIC Report, Introduction, paragraphs 18–21.
6. Synoptic Overview of the HRVIC Report, Chapter 3, paragraphs 95–100.
7. Dr. Ransome Kuti brought a petition on behalf of his family against a number of military generals including president Obasanjo alleging that he and certain members of his family were assaulted, tortured, and their land confiscated by the military because of his stance against the form of government.
8. Synoptic Overview of the HRVIC Report, Foreword, paragraph 1.38.
9. Synoptic Overview of the HRVIC Report, Foreword, paragraph 1.43.
10. Synoptic Overview of the HRVIC Report, Foreword, paragraph 1.33.
11. Synoptic Overview of the HRVIC Report, Introduction, paragraph 18–19.
12. *Today*, 2–8, January, 2000.
13. William Shabas, "The Sierra Leone Truth and Reconciliation Commission," in *Transitional Justice in the Twenty-First Century, Beyond Truth Versus Justice,* ed. Naomi Roht-Arriaza and Javier Mariezcurrena (Cambridge: Cambridge University Press, 2006).

Appendix A

Research Methods

INTRODUCTION

Hoddinott and Devereux (1993) in *Fieldwork in Developing Countries* advocate a very simple and realistic approach to methodology. They argue that equal consideration of the context and methodology of research is critical for making a good assessment of the research process. Cognizant of the transparency that such an approach generates, I have assessed my research methods according to two congruous principles of 'reflexivity' and 'problem consciousness.' Reflexivity questions the scientific illusion of the 'third person' in research.[1] Consciousness of the problem calls for exposing the strengths and weaknesses of research by illuminating the assumptions, prejudices, and difficulties encountered in the research process.[2]

Scheman emphasizes the need to clarify the identity of the researcher. Responsible research reporting requires the questioning of the 'I' who constructs the questions out of the problems that arise, the 'I' out of whose experience the problems arise and the 'I' from whose perspective the questions or problems are salient.[3] In reflecting on the 'I' within my research process, I confirm that research is a personal activity. This is least because the way my research was conducted, including my very identity as a person, determined the answers given to me by respondents, informational resources provided by my host and home communities, as well as the tangential issues that I noticed to be relevant to my research topic. These steps in research, to a large extent, cannot be replicated. Williams asserts:

> In doing fieldwork . . . my work is a cultural performance. From the stream of action I encounter, I select bits and pieces. It is like Clifford Geertz's (1973) description of ethnography. Summarized very crudely, the fieldworker pulls

together the bits and pieces of the so-called actors' constructions of what is going on to create her own constructions.[4]

Therefore, the reality is that I, as a researcher, am a social being with affiliations by nature and nurture. These affiliations have influenced how I feel and understand the events of my research because my consciousness is the primary mechanism through which my research analysis is conducted and "there is no method or technique of doing research other than through the medium of the researcher."[5]

The first difficulties with my research were encountered at the preparatory stage of my interview process. To date, no academic paper has been written about the Nigerian Human Rights Violations Investigation Commission (HRVIC). This significant absence of literature was both a motivating factor and a deprivation in my research. In preparing for my fieldwork, I could only use the materials written on other truth commissions. The significant realization in my preparatory readings was my limitation in resources, both in time and finances, to undertake the sort of extensive research necessary to fully explore the unique features of the Nigerian case. Thus, I made use of research techniques that are, perhaps, not the quintessential template for fieldwork but which proved feasible and to a degree successful in the elite-type interviews that I undertook. This approach, as argued by Schatzman and Strauss (1973), presents the researcher with her most effective tool as methodological approaches should be employed in terms of their pertinence to the problem or issue under investigation rather than concern for orthodox frameworks.

CHOOSING A RESEARCH TOPIC

Since no true academic pursuit is initiated without any trace of personal significance, the reasons for my choice of topic are not atypical. My topic presented itself to me at the meeting of my personal experience as an Igbo of Nigeria and an academic trajectory that has taken me through Philosophy, Politics, African Studies, and Development Studies.

I grew up in a town that was riddled with metaphoric references to the traumatic experience of the Nigerian-Biafran war without any direct accounting for "those days." For example, the identification and identity of age grades around the period were couched in memories of the war. Age grade titles are picked at the age of eighteen when a boy is initiated into manhood. Thus, eighteen years after the war, those born during the war were called Osondu which means 'those who ran the race of life' and the subsequent age group was called Ogueri, 'those who were not eaten by war.' Northerners were perceived with an enmity unlike any other directed towards Nigeria's other multiple ethnicities. For example, I remember having an initial distrust of my northern classmates when I went to a national boarding school at the age of eleven, a distrust whose origin I could not pinpoint. This age grade naming pattern highlights the methods of incorporating historical events into tradition, the process for dealing with violence and past traumas, and the making of history through customizing memories that are intentionally or unintentionally forgotten or remembered. Such articulation and sensitivities naturally piqued my curiosity regarding the war but also framed my youthful understanding of Nigeria politics as the politics of the 'guilty other' and 'innocent us.'

As an undergraduate student reading Politics, Philosophy, and African Studies, my personal curiosity in many ways informed my intellectual biography, crystallizing into an undergraduate thesis on the legacy of the war for contemporary Nigerian politics. Though an arduous process of personal ideological (re)formation, I was able to create the necessary distance between me, as an academic, and the emotional sensitivities of the Igbos in general. However, after conducting that study, I found that the sensitivities regarding the war were not particular to the Igbos. The Ijaws, Kalabaris, Efiks, Hausas, Yorubas, etc. all had long held sensitive perceptions of the war. What is most characteristic is the way in which all the varied groups defined their case against some implicit criticism of the other. I articulated these sensitivities as the manifestation of an unresolved past now under constant re-formulation and politicization by the elite seeking mass support for the sake of contemporary "spoils politics."

Stumbling upon the Ohaneze petition to the HRVIC while conducting the research for my undergraduate thesis, I immediately recognized the significance of the Commission. For the first time, the 1966 coups, the pogroms, and issues regarding the war such as the Asaba massacre, which were never explored in any legal process, were presented before a quasi-judicial enquiry. Additionally, the nature of the Commission as a product of Nigeria's first democratic rule in sixteen years and third period of democratic rule in all of its independent history, and its potential impact on the continent given the debates around South Africa's TRC strengthened its appeal as a subject of study.

All these issues not only raised political questions of how a supposedly non-politicized commission of truth and reconciliation, modeled after South Africa's TRC, would fare in the face of the very politicized discourse of 'the civil war' and ethnicity in Nigeria, but also highlighted the ongoing (re)construction of historical memory through present actions. Philosophically, it raised questions of what justice, truth, and reconciliation entailed in this instance, to what extent these concepts were individually contested and collectively compatible, and what applied justice meant for societies in transition. I was disappointed to find an absolute silence on the question of Nigeria's truth commission on the part of both domestic and international academics, and so I was challenged to venture into this field by examining how the HRVIC fared as a truth commission in Nigeria.

Therefore, both personal interest and sufficient unexplored information to pursue my investigation were the founding reasons for my research topic.

THE RESEARCH STRATEGY: FORMULATION AND APPLICATION

Due to the nature of discourses such as ethnicity and justice, my research strategy could not rely on quantitative techniques. Quantitative surveys of people's philosophies, memories, and notions of justice cannot easily be strictly codified. Codification of such responses may produce precise statistical calculations but will effectively eradicate the richness of the nuances that are encountered in such topics.[6] In fact, Lockwood argues that particular tools of research can be found to be quite irrelevant while a researcher is in the field.[7]

In the first formulation of my research strategy, I explored the possibility of using quantitative methods in my research. The goal was to create a survey to gauge public opinion in the post-HRVIC era. This was to be conducted through a random sampling of neighborhoods and homes in three of the five cities where the Commission sat and in three other randomly selected cities where the Commission did not sit. With twenty-five surveys per city, I would collect data from 150 respondents. On reflection, I opted out of this approach as it failed to meet several statistical standards. For example, 150 respondents selected only in cities necessarily exclude the larger percentage of the population who live in rural areas. People in rural areas may be more likely to have stronger opinions with regard to the question of ethnicity because of the lack of exposure to diversity, which a metropolitan environment provides. Safety precautions and financial constraints necessitated refraining from going into rural areas. My confinement to cities possibly increased the probability that my respondents would have particular (perhaps city prevalent) opinions. The opinions of 150 people in the urban areas cannot be used to make a credible statistical inference to a population of approximately 126 million people, 80 percent of whom live in rural areas. Given this challenge and the already mentioned benefits of adopting the qualitative approach in finding answers to my type of questions, I placed all my methods within the qualitative camp.

My first challenge in adopting a qualitative approach was the issue of emic versus etic approaches to fieldwork whereby the researcher is either an insider or outsider in relation to the research location. The emic approach to research is necessary for intuitive and empathetic understanding of cultural perspectives essential for conducting effective fieldwork and also serves as a valuable source of inspiration for etic hypotheses. The etic system, which uses conceptual schemes and categories that are widely accepted or meaningful in academia, is important for comparative analyses.[8] Lett argues that any claim of the etic approach to generate objective knowledge and thus superior to emic systems is illusionary. Rather, the etic approach is important as a way of penetrating, discovering, and elucidating emic systems.[9] While in Nigeria and during the analysis and writing stage, I simultaneously remained conscious of the specific features of Nigeria's truth commission and the paradigmatic categories formulated from comparative analyses of other truth commissions.

Furthermore, I am Nigerian and thus, was acculturated to the research location. Yet, having lived outside the country for almost a decade beginning with the key formative years of adulthood, there were important sensibilities that I did not share. I was in a sense both an outsider and insider to the research location. Rasavi affirms that even those who identify as insiders are rarely complete insiders. Many a time, researchers are urban middle class individuals working with residents of slum or village communities.[10] Therefore, members of the same nationality can possess distinct spatial identities. Since most cultural anthropologists encourage the achievement of both views, I saw this as advantageous.[11] To be consistent with already posited arguments, I adopted the etic approach in so far as it guided logical rather than empirical analyses. Therefore, the etic view was to guide the relationship between the information obtained and the conclusions arrived therefrom in terms of falsifiability, comprehensiveness, and logical consistency rather than the replicability of my research. Similarly, the emic approach is preceded with the caveat that any posited cultural explanations are informed but subjective perceptions of cultural occurrences.

With approximately two months to conduct my fieldwork, my research was based on general literature on truth commissions, elite-type interviews, and research documents (including copies of petitions, transcripts of the public hearing, newspaper articles, and government documents). I first conducted the pre-fieldwork reading in Oxford in order to draft my research questions. Given the absence of literature on the Nigerian truth commission, I spent most of the time reading the literature on the South African, Chilean, and Argentine cases. Fortunately, the presence of one of the commissioners of the Nigerian truth commission at Oxford made it possible not only to gain some immediate insights into the Commission but also to make contacts in Nigeria.

My research questions began with looking at the HRVIC as a truth commission and asking to what extent it was effective as a panel aimed at airing human rights violations through truth telling and reconciling warring parties.

The unit of analysis was the Ohaneze petition. My preparatory questions were thematically as follows: To what extent was the Commission successful in the absence of an amnesty incentive?; Is a truth commission the best way to deal with the ethnic conflict in Nigeria's past and present?; To what extent was the state sensitive to the people's notion of justice; and how did the people interpret the government's motivation in setting up a truth commission in guiding the writing of their petitions? Basic fieldwork strategy was as the follows:

a. Acquisition of the relevant documents presented at the Commission.
b. Elite-type interviews in Abuja and Enugu where the Ohaneze case and the Arewa counter case were heard. Interview questions were to vary slightly with respect to:
   i. Leaders of regional/ethnic organizations. These interviews aimed to provide the nuanced perspectives of people with regard to the Commission and its goals.
   ii. Members of the Commission. These interviews were aimed at procuring information regarding the rubric for the Commission's recommendations since they are not made according to the retributive codes of the Constitution. These interviews were also aimed at examining the nature of the relationship between the state and the Commission.
   iii. Lawyers who represented both case and counter-case in order to acquire their analysis and synthesis of the distinct natures of case preparation for a trial and for a Truth and Reconciliation process. This is necessary because the distinction between HRVIC as a commission of enquiry and HRVIC as a trial commission with limited powers became blurred during the sittings. This could have informed the way truth was told which would consequently inform the reconciliation process.
c. Media archival research was to be conducted in the two cities in order to explore popular opinions during the HRVIC public hearings and the post-HRVIC period.

After pre-fieldwork discussions with Father Kukah, the aforementioned commissioner of the Nigerian truth commission, I became aware of ethnic petitions generated by the Ohaneze petition. Most notable among them were the Arewa response to the Ohaneze petition and the South-South petition engendered by the attitude of the Commission to the Ohaneze-Arewa confrontation.[12] With this new information, I added questions regarding the conduct of the ethno-political organizations in relation to their counterparts and the Commission's response to the ethnic controversy. These were the first of many questions that would arise during the interview and information-analysis process.

With about eight weeks to conduct my fieldwork, I planned to share the time equally between the cities of Enugu, Abuja, and Lagos in Nigeria where I would interview the Commission's staff and the main contenders, on the issue of ethnicity and war-related but not war violations. Additionally, while in each area, I would spend some time collecting textual materials pertinent to the research. This strategy did not work out exactly as planned. Some of the respondents had traveled to their ancestral homes during the period that I was in the area or were completely out of the country. I gained an audience with the leaders of the Ohaneze and the South-South but not the Arewa organization. On the other hand, I interviewed the key witness of the Arewa but not the other two groups. The only respondent that I followed out of my stated locations was the chairman of the Commission, Justice Oputa, who had retired and was permanently residing in his ancestral home. Following the advice of Father Kukah while in Oxford, I bought a bottle of Cognac as a customary courtesy, which was well received on meeting Justice Oputa. The discomfort I felt at showing up with no previous appointment dissipated as I realized that appointments were not necessary in all cases. Unable to acclimatize to the idea of not making appointments, I tried to make appointments and only showed up without one when such attempts failed. What seemed most important for many of these elite respondents were personal references.

My interviews were conducted with a structured set of questions but were open ended to allow for dialogue and any information that I did not directly seek but which may be relevant to my study.[13] I sometimes struck up informal conversations on university campuses, buses, and with host-families to gauge the perceptions of ordinary citizens on the Commission. I conducted elite-type interviews, because these groups were more informed about the nature and complexities of the Commission and the petitions. These respondents were sampled in terms of ethnic representation and I was aware of the absence of women's opinions on the Commission. This absence expressly reflects the domination of men in Nigeria's politics, ethnic or otherwise.

Goward's (1984) caveat that elite interviews may be very difficult particularly for student researchers, especially in terms of access, proved to be the case for me. This was not only because I was a student but because of my age and sex. In the three locations where I conducted interviews, there seemed to be no sense of urgency or order in many offices. Some of the respondents made me wait in their office throughout the whole day to see them or return the next day. Observing the process by which people were seen, status, age, and sex seemed to coincide with the order in which waiting visitors were met and attended to. As such, being from Oxford provided me with status but my age and sex detracted from the importance attributed to me.

This elite-interview approach generated further challenges. First, utilizing a "snowball" strategy proved successful among the Ohaneze group but was unsuccessful among the Arewa group and the South-South group. Thus, my intention to interview equal numbers of people on each side was not possible. This is particularly key for the Arewa group who presented the main case in response to the Ohaneze petition. However, a comprehensive interview with the key witness for the group proved much more rewarding than the interviews I conducted with some of the Ohaneze members. The success of the snowball effect among Ohaneze was insightful in providing me with the reasons for my lack of success among the others. I was usually introduced over the phone to the next respondent as "our daughter who is conducting a research on the petition." Therefore, there was a conflating of identities between the researched and the researcher by the researched.[14] Being "our daughter" simultaneously gave me access and generated expectations. In some ways I felt like an impostor who was privy to private information. In response, I consistently emphasized my conduct as a researcher rather than a "young Igbo woman."

Second, although my ethnic identity proved advantageous in some cases, in many other ways, it was an obstacle. Sarsby argues that those who argue against 'insiders' working in his/her own society ignore the "tension between the need for both empathy and detachment."[15] At a particular interview, a respondent, frustrated with my lack of emotional commiseration with his outrage regarding the war atrocities threw a book at me screaming "Are you not Igbo? It does not seem to me that you know of these atrocities so you should go and read up on what they have done to us." This focus on my ethnic identity was very challenging for me.

Given that I lived outside of Nigeria and did not have the accent of a resident Nigerian, there was a distinction between the way I was treated when I spoke and when I subsequently gave my name. This is because my name alerted people to my national and ethnic identity. On interviewing an Arewa member, I was at first mistaken for a foreign student coming from Oxford. In this position, I was briefly shown the unpublished report of the truth commission, which legally should not be in the public domain. At this juncture, I was told that "a Yoruba man set up a commission being chaired by an Igbo and we [which could mean Northerners or Hausa-Fulanis but referring to the ethno-political group represented by the Arewa] are supposed to fold our hands and watch?" At the end of my interview, I was asked to write my name and number for contact purposes, as my name will be passed along to other Arewa members. I was also given some of these names but my attempts to set up appointments met with failure. In one scenario, a secretary set up an appointment for me with a vital member of the Arewa and after the appointment was set up, I asked to give my name and number. However, calling to confirm on the morning of the interview, I was told that he had traveled to his ancestral home and on a third call that he had been urgently called to Saudi Arabia and there were no ideas regarding the date of his return. I could only interpret this as a refusal to meet with me because "s/he has traveled" is a well-known excuse in Nigeria for refusing to see a guest. Furthermore, in trying to contact an already interviewed respondent, I met a brick wall in the form of the secretary. These secretaries served as "gatekeepers" who controlled my access to respondents and, in most cases, it seemed that their decisions were based on consultations with respondents.[16]

The imbalance in interviews led to a more critical examination of the Ohaneze group relative to the Arewa group. However, the procurement of both the Ohaneze petition and the Arewa response provided enough information for a sufficient analysis of both in relation to the Commission and each other.

Documents and general literature filled the gaps in my interview process and provided much of the missing information that I sought from respondents. Thus, it proved invaluable to the compromises made due to the constraints I faced.[17] The procurement of archival texts through public systems such as libraries and media archives was obstructed by the request to provide ridiculous amounts of money in "user fees" which meant some form of bribery. Thus, many of the documents that I intended to get in the libraries were obtained from respondents who had copies in their possession. On the other hand, general literature on truth commissions was easily available through the Oxford library system.

By the end of my fieldwork, the need for further research was obvious. Indeed such a predicament is the norm in most fieldwork situations.[18] For example, initial analysis of interviews hinted at intra-ethnic disagreements about the prayers of the petition, the legitimacy of the representing organizations and the internal class dynamics of the representing organization. Resource constraints compromised my ability to ascertain more palpable information regarding this issue since I could not go back to the field. Instead, I sought to find ways of answering some of my fieldwork-engendered questions. This was only successful with two key respondents who were serendipitously in the West at the time, that is, Father Kukah and Mrs. Uwandu. Access to Nigeria through phone-calls and emails failed abysmally. I have noted these issues in the study to make readers aware of the existence of these intra-ethnic tensions. Generally, I have re-channeled the "incomplete" nature of my fieldwork by including fieldwork and analysis-generated questions in my conclusion, simultaneously positioning some of my conclusions about my research within this context and making the case for the need for further research.

INFORMATION ANALYSIS AND THE WRITING PROCESS

In analyzing documents, Tosh argues that it is necessary to be conscious of the significance of documentary texts and the process by which they are produced.[19] Engaging with the textual constructions of documentary texts, I have placed the documents within the wider socio-political contexts out of which they arise and to which they address. For example, reading the two official documents mandating the truth commission from this paradigm reveals the differences in the texts as evidence of the negotiations between the government and the truth commission contained within compromises made by the government in response to public opinion and criticism.[20]

Additionally, secondary texts such as academic literature on truth commissions in general were invaluable. They provided a much wider context and frame within which Nigeria's Commission could be more universally assessed. These texts greatly enriched the information-analysis stage of my research. However, they could not be used as a complete means for comparison since some of the issues raised in interviews were unique to the Nigerian reality while the secondary texts explored truth commissions theoretically or referred to the realities of other truth commissions in their analysis.

Interviews were conducted in English and information from interviews was stored through note-taking and, in cases where it was allowed, through tape-recordings. The teasing out of sentiments through speech in some parts confirmed documentary texts and in other parts conflicted if not contradicted written texts. For example, the claim that the Ohaneze petition was written for posterity were emphasized by some Ohaneze respondents and completely sidelined by others. The tension and disagreements that were obscured in the petition were illuminated in interviews. As with texts, speech is a deliberate action designed to have deliberate consequences. It is not as fine-tuned as texts and could produce nuances that can illuminate the process of text production. In analyzing the interviews, I examined the ways in which and stages where opinions appear in texts.[21] This approach resulted in the highlighting of issues that were not presented officially through the petitions. In a more expanded analysis, I would further explore the reasons why such issues were not presented officially.

In terms of structure, I realized that without any previous academic literature on the HRVIC, I could not present the ethnic debates in a text that merely assumes knowledge of the HRVIC process in general. This necessitated a restructuring whereby a whole chapter is dedicated to a largely expository overview of the HRVIC process. The goal of the overall project was to create an academic introduction to the HRVIC question. With plans for possible publication, I hoped to engender further research.

Lessons from and lapses in my analysis of the Nigerian HRVIC highlight two important issues. First, the impenetrability of the fortress of the sectarian elite who guard the ethnic establishment from investigations into authentic popular opinion in Nigeria unwittingly points to the need to explore the politics of the emerging elite along generation lines and the resulting intra-ethnic tension. Secondly, further studies on truth commissions need to be contextualized, not only in historical contexts that ethnic politics and the nature of truth commissions naturally demand, but within the different discourses of contemporary politics. For example, understanding the relationship between democratization, among neo-liberal foundations of globalization, and the spread of truth commissions can provide some insights into the appeal and or lack thereof for the diverse interests that support or denounce its use. It will also shed some light on the potential for truth commissions in the African context.

ETHICAL AND POLITICAL ISSUES

Asking questions regarding a Commission whose report has not been published for political reasons made a few respondents suspicious. To ensure that both supporters and detractors of the HRVIC in the discourse did not see me as an activist seeking to buttress the perspective of any one side, I was very careful to explain the nature of my research and the ultimate outcome of my fieldwork as an academic text. I am aware that my success or failure in clarifying my role within the research site cannot really be measured. Nevertheless, it was necessary, for ethical purposes that supporters were made aware of the purely academic nature of my research.

Second, I have also endeavored to present, as faithfully as I can, evidence as obtained, making distinctions between individual opinions and official position of organizations and maintaining the anonymity of those who made such requests. Finally, having stated the limitations of objectivity and yet analyzed information as logically as I can, I still remain conscious of those subjective potholes that can only be pointed out by readers. I believe that overall, this study has created a foundation, through the questions it poses, for the necessary debate regarding alternative means of resolving Nigeria's ethnic problems.

DISSEMINATION

In appreciation of the goodwill extended towards me during my research process and the need to send my findings to those for whom the study has been conducted, I intend to send copies of my study to Ohaneze, Arewa, and the members of the Commission whom I interviewed. Additionally, following Wilson's (1993) argument that disseminating should be carried out after the risk of doing so has been well evaluated, I have ensured that none of the information and conclusions in this study pose any threat of negative repercussions for my respondents. My conclusions encourage more serious thinking on the role of the state and ethnic identity in the socio-political life of Nigerians and how the conflicts generated by the state as an entity and ethnicity as a politicized discourse can be resolved. My hope is that at least Nigerian intellectuals and university scholars can take up the question. Thus, I also intend to send a copy of this study to the library of the University of Nigeria.

CONCLUSION

Despite the challenges that occurred during fieldwork and the limitations of the research process in general, the detailed reflexive approach taken in accounting for my research methods provides the logical link between the information obtained and the conclusions made. Thus, those limitations do not and cannot discount the conclusions presented herein.

NOTES

1. See Naomi Scheman, "Unavoidability of Gender," in *Women, Knowledge and Reality. Explorations of Feminist Philosophy,* ed. Marilyn Pearsall and Ann Garry (London: Unwin Hyman, 1989); Liz Stanley and Sue Wise, *Breaking Out Again: Feminist Ontology and Epistemology*, 2nd Edition (London: Routledge, 1993); Ann Oakley, *Experiments in Knowing. Gender and Method in Social Sciences* (Cambridge: Polity Press, 2000).
2. See John Hoddinott, "Fieldwork under Time Constraints," in *Fieldwork in Developing Countries*, ed. S. Devereux and J. Hoddinott (Colorado: Lynne Rienner Publishers, 1993); Tim May, *Social Research: Issues, Methods and Process,* 2nd edition (Buckingham and Philadelphia: Open University Press, 1997).
3. Scheman, "Unavoidability of Gender."
4. Anne Williams, *Rhetoric as Cultural Performance,* unpublished paper (BSA Medical Sociology Group Conference, 1983), 2.
5. Stanley and Wise, *Breaking Out Again: Feminist Ontology and Epistemology.*
6. Bruce Berg, *Qualitative Research Methods: For the Social Sciences* (Boston: Allyn and Bacon, 1988); Herbert Rubin and Irene Rubin, *Qualitative Interviewing: The Art of Hearing Data* (Thousand Oaks, California: Sage Publications, 1995); May, *Social Research.*

7. Matthew Lockwood, "Facts or Fiction? Fieldwork Relationships and the Nature of Data," in *Fieldwork in Developing Countries*, ed. S. Devereux and J. Hoddinott (Colorado: Lynne Rienner Publishers, 1993).

8. James Lett, "Emics and Etics: Notes on the Epistemology of Anthropology," in *Emics and Etics: The Insider/Outsider Debate*, ed. *Thomas* Headland Thomas, Kenneth Pike, and Marvin Harris (Newbury Park: Sage Publications,1990); Clifford Geertz, *The Interpretation of Cultures* (New York: Basic Books, 1973); R.F. Ellen, "Introduction," in *Ethnographic Research. A Guide to General Conduct*, ed. R.F. Ellen (London: Academic Press Ltd., 1984).

9. Lett, "Emics and Etics."

10. S. Rasavi, "Fieldwork in a Familiar Setting: The Role of Politics at the National, Communal, and Household Levels," in *Fieldwork in Developing Countries*, ed. S. Devereux and J. Hoddinott (Colorado: Lynne Rienner Publishers, 1993).

11. Lett, "Emics and Etics,"133; Ellen, "Introduction," 129.

12. See chapters three and four.

13. Rubin and Rubin, *Qualitative Interviewing*.

14. Nicola Goward, "Personal Interaction and Adjustment," in *Ethnographic Research. A Guide to General Conduct*, ed. R.F. Ellen (London: Academic Press Ltd., 1984).

15. Jacquie Sarsby, "Special Problems of Fieldwork in Familiar Settings," in *Ethnographic Research. A Guide to General Conduct*, ed. R.F. Ellen (London: Academic Press Ltd., 1984), 129.

16. Judith Bell and Clive Opie, *Learning from Research: Getting more from your Data* (Buckingham and Philadelphia: Open University Press, 2002); Paul Oliver, *The Student's Guide to Research Ethics* (Maidenhead and Philadelphia: Open University Press, 2003).

17. John Hoddinott, "Fieldwork under Time Constraints."

18. S. Devereux and J. Hoddinott J., "Introduction," in *Fieldwork in Developing Countries*, ed. S. Devereux and J. Hoddinott (Colorado: Lynne Rienner Publishers, 1993).

19. John Tosh, *The Pursuit of History: Aims Methods and New Directions in the Study of Modern History,* 3rd Edition (London: Longman, 2002).

20. See chapter two.

21. Rubin and Rubin, *Qualitative Interviewing.*

Appendix B

S. I. 8 of 1999 **B37**

TRIBUNALS OF INQUIRY ACT
(CAP 447 LFN)
COMMENCEMENT: 7TH JUNE 1999

INSTRUMENT CONSTITUTING A JUDICIAL COMMISSION OF INQUIRY FOR THE INVESTIGATION OF HUMAN RIGHTS VIOLATIONS

In exercise of the powers conferred upon me by section 1 of the Tribunals of Inquiry Act and of all other powers enabling me in that behalf, **I, OLUSEGUN OBASANJO,** President, Commander-in-Chief of the Armed Forces of the Federal Republic of Nigerian, hereby constitute and appoint a Judicial Commission of Inquiry for the investigation of human rights violations with terms of reference hereinafter appearing:

AND for that purpose, I appoint –

Hon. Justice Chukwudifu Oputa (rtd)	-	Chairman
Abubakar Ali Kura Michika	-	Member
Mallam Mamman Daura	-	Member
Rev. Matthew H. Kukah	-	Member

Mrs Elizabeth Pam	-	Member
Dr Tunji Abayomi	-	Member
Mrs Modupe Areola	-	Member
Mr N.B. Dambatta, mni	-	Secretary

to be members of the Judicial Commission with full powers and authority to hold public hearing but without prejudice to the exercise of the powers conferred under the proviso to section 1(2)(d) of the said Act:

Terms of Reference

The Judicial Commission shall –

(a) ascertain or establish the causes, nature and extent of human rights violations or abuses with particular reference to all known or suspected cases of mysterious deaths and assassinations or attempted assassinations committed in Nigeria between the 1st day of January 1984 and the 28th of May, 1999;

(b) identify the person or persons, authorities, institutions or organizations which may be held accountable for such mysterious deaths, assassinations or attempted assassinations or other violations or abuses of human rights and determine the motives of the violations or abuses, the victims and circumstances thereof and the effect on such victims or the society generally of the atrocities;

(c) determine whether such abuses or violations were the product of deliberate State policy or the policy of any of its organs or institutions or whether they arose from abuses by State officials of their office or whether they were the acts of any political organizations, liberation movements or other groups or individuals;

(d) recommend measures which may be taken whether judicial, administrative, legislative or institutional to redress the injustices of the past and prevent or forestall future violation or abuses of human rights;

(e) make any other recommendations which are, in the opinion of the Judicial Commission, in the public interest and are necessitated by the evidence.

AND I hereby direct the Judicial Commission to submit its interim reports to me from time to time but shall, in any case, submit its final report not later than ninety days from the date of its first public sitting or within such extended period as may be authorized by me in writing.

GIVEN AND ISSUED under my hand at Abuja this 7th day of June 1999.

SIGNED
OLUSEGUN OBASANJO, GCFR,
President, Commander-in-Chief
of the Armed Forces of the
Federal Republic of Nigeria.

Appendix C

S.I. of 1999

TRIBUNALS OF INQUIRY ACT
(CAP 447 LFN)
COMMENCEMENT: 4TH OCTOBER 1999

AMENDMENT OF INSTRUMENT CONSTITUTING A JUDICIAL COMMISSION OF INQUIRY FOR THE INVESTIGATION OF HUMAN RIGHTS VIOLATIONS

In exercise of the powers conferred upon me by section 1 of the Tribunals of Inquiry Act and of all other powers enabling me in that behalf, **I, OLUSEGUN OBASANJO,** President, Commander-in-Chief of the Armed Forces of the Federal Republic of Nigerian, hereby amend Statutory Instrument No. 8 of 1999 by which I constituted and appointed a Judicial Commission of Inquiry for the investigation of human rights violations with terms of reference hereinafter appearing, as follows:-

AND for that purpose, I appoint –

Hon. Justice Chukwudifu Oputa (rtd)	-	Chairman
Dr. Mudiaga Odje, SAN, OFR	-	Member
Rev. Matthew H. Kukah	-	Member

Barr. Bala Ngilari	-	Member
Mrs. Elizabeth Pam	-	Member
Mrs. Modupe Areola	-	Member
Alhaji Lawal Bamali	-	Member
Mr N.B. Dambatta, mni	-	Secretary

to be members of the Judicial Commission with full powers and authority to hold public hearing but without prejudice to the exercise of the powers conferred under the proviso to section 1(2)(d) of the said Act:

Terms of Reference

The Judicial Commission shall –

(a) ascertain or establish the causes, nature and extent of all gross violations of human rights committed in Nigeria between the 15th day of January 1966 and the 28th day of May, 1999;
(b) identify the person or persons, authorities, institutions or organizations which may be held accountable for such gross violations of human rights and determine the motives of the violations or abuses, the victims and circumstances thereof and the effect on such victims and the society generally of the atrocities;
(c) determine whether such abuses or violations were the product of deliberate State policy or the policy of any of its organs or institutions or whether they arose from abuses by State officials of their office or whether they were the acts of any political organizations, liberation movements or other groups or individuals;
(d) recommend measures which may be taken whether judicial, administrative, legislative or institutional to redress the injustices of the past and prevent or forestall future violation or abuses of human rights;
(e) make any other recommendations which are, in the opinion of the Judicial Commission, in the public interest and are necessitated by the evidence;
(f) to receive any legitimate financial or other assistance from whatever source which may aid and facilitate the realization of its objectives.

AND I hereby direct the Judicial Commission to submit its interim reports to me from time to time but shall, in any case, submit its final report not later than one year from the date of its first public sitting or within such extended period as may be authorized by me in writing.

GIVEN AND ISSUED under my hand at Abuja this 4th day of October 1999.

SIGNED
OLUSEGUN OBASANJO, GCFR,
President, Commander-in-Chief
of the Armed Forces of the
Federal Republic of Nigeria.

Appendix D

Table comparing religion and ethnicity of commissioners.

Name	*Sex*	*Religion*	*State/Ethnicity*
Justice Chukwudifu S. Oputa (rtd)	Male	Christian	Imo/Igbo
Dr Mudiaga Odje	Male	Christian	Delta/Urhobo
Reverend Matthew H. Kukah	Male	Christian	Kaduna/Ikulu
Barrister Bala Ngilari	Male	Christian	Adamawa/-
Mrs Elizabeth Pam	Female	Christian	Plateau State/-
Mrs Modupe Areola	Female	Christian	Ogun/Yoruba
Alhaji Lawal Bamali	Male	Muslim	Kaduna/Hausa
Mr N.B. Dambatta, mni	Male	Christian	Kano/-
Abubakar Tura Michika (Replaced)	Male	Muslim	-/Hausa
Mallam Mamman Daura (Replaced)	Male	Muslim	-/Hausa
Dr. Tunji Abayomi (Replaced)	Male	Christian	-/Yoruba

Bibliography

Books and Journal Articles

Ademoyega, Adewale. '*Why We Struck: The Story of the First Nigerian Coup*,' Ibadan, Nigeria: Evans Brothers (Nigerian Publishers), 1981.

Amadiume, Ifi. "The Politics of Memory: Biafra and Intellectual Responsibility," in Amadiume Ifi, & Abdullahi An-Na'im, (eds) *The Politics of Memory: Truth, Healing and Social Justice*, London and New York: Zed Books, 2000.

Amadiume, Ifi and An-Na'im, Abdullahi. "Introduction," in Amadiume Ifi, & An-Na'im Abdullahi, (eds) *The Politics of Memory: Truth, Healing and Social Justice*, London and New York: Zed Books, 2000.

Asmal K., Asmal L., and Roberts R. *Reconciliation through Truth: A Reckoning of Apartheid's Criminal Governance*, 2nd Edition, Oxford: James Currey, 1997.

Bardhan, Pranab. *Method in the Madness? A Political Economy Analysis of Ethnic Conflicts in Less Developed Countries*, Center for International and Development Economics Research. Working Paper No. C96-070, University of California, Berkeley, 1996.

Barghava, Rajeev. "Restoring Decency to Barbaric Societies," in Rotberg R. & Thompson D. (eds) *Truth V. Justice*, New Jersey: Princeton University Press, 1989.

——. "The Moral Justifications of Truth Commissions," in Villa-Vicencio C., and Verwoerd W., (eds) *Looking Back Reaching Forward: Reflections on the Truth and Reconciliation Commission of South Africa*, Cape Town: University of Cape Town Press, 2000.

Barry, Brian. *Theories of Justice*, Hertfordshire: Harvester and Wheatsheaf, 1989.

Bell, Judith and Opie, Clive. "*Learning from Research: Getting more from your Data*," Buckingham and Philadelphia: Open University Press, 2002.

Berg, Bruce. *Qualitative Research Methods: For the Social Sciences*, Boston: Allyn and Bacon, 1988.

Campbell, Tom. *Justice*, London: Macmillan Press, 1988.

Christie, Kenneth. *The South African Truth Commission,* New York: St Martin's Press, 2000.

de Lange, Johnny. "The Historical Contexts, Legal Origins and Philosophical Foundations of the South African Truth and Reconciliation Commission," in Villa-Vicencio C., and Verwoerd W., (eds) *Looking Back Reaching Forward: Reflections on the Truth and Reconciliation Commission of South Africa,* Cape Town: University of Cape Town Press, 2000.

Devereux, S. and Hoddinott, J. "Introduction," in Devereux S., and Hoddinott J., (eds) *Fieldwork in Developing Countries,* Colorado: Lynne Rienner Publishers Inc, 1993.

du Toit, Andre. "The Moral Foundations of the South African TRC: Truth as Acknowledgment and Justice as Recognition," in Rotberg R. & Thompson D. (eds) *Truth V. Justice,* New Jersey: Princeton University Press, 2000.

Ellen, R.F. "Introduction," in Ellen R.F., (ed) *Ethnographic Research. A Guide to General Conduct,* London: Academic Press Ltd, 1984.

Fraser, Nancy . "From Redistribution to Recognition? Dilemmas of Justice in a 'Post-socialist' Age, *New Left Review* 212," in *Feminism and Politics,* edited by Anne Phillips. Oxford: Oxford University Press, 1998.

Gallie, W.B. "Essentially Contested Concepts," *Proceedings of the Aristotelian Society,* 56, 1956.

Geertz, Clifford. *The Interpretation of Cultures,* New York: Basic Books, 1973.

Gibson, James L. "Truth, Justice, and Reconciliation: Judging the Fairness of Amnesty in South Africa," *American Journal of Political Science* 46(2002): 540–556.

Goldstone, Richard. "Foreword" in Villa-Vicencio Charles and Verwoerd Wilhelm (eds.) in *Looking Back, Reaching Forward: Reflections on the Truth and Reconciliation Commissions of South Africa,* Cape Town: University of Cape Town Press, 2000.

Goward, Nicola. "Personal Interaction and Adjustment," in *Ethnographic Research. A Guide to General Conduct,* edited by R. F. Ellen. London: Academic Press Ltd., 1984.

Grandin, Greg. "The Instruction of Great Catastrophe: Truth Commissions, National History, and State Formation in Argentina, Chile and Guatemala," *The American Historical Review* 110, no. 1: 3(2005).

Graybill, Lynn . "*Truth and Reconciliation in South Africa. Miracle or Model?,*" London: Lynne Rienner Publishers, 2002.

Graybill, Lynn and Lanegran, Kimberly. "Introduction to Special Issue on TRCs: Truth, Justice, and Reconciliation in Africa: Issues and Cases," *African Studies Quarterly* 8, no.1, [online]: <http://web.africa.ufl.edu/asq/v8/v8i1a1.htm> (accessed February 28, 2007).

Gutmann, Amy & Thompson, Dennis. "The Moral Foundations of Truth Commissions," in *Truth V. Justice,* edited by Rotberg R. & Thompson D. New Jersey: Princeton University Press, 2000.

Hayner, Priscilla B. "Fifteen Truth Commissions–1974 to 1994: A Comparative Study," *Human Rights Quarterly* 16, no. 4(1994): 597–655.

———. "Same Species, Different Animal: How South Africa Compares to Truth Commissions World-wide," in *Looking Back Reaching Forward: Reflections on the Truth and Reconciliation Commission of South Africa*, edited by C. Villa-Vicencio and W. Verwoerd. Cape Town: University of Cape Town Press, 2000.

Hoddinott, John. "Fieldwork under Time Constraints," in *Fieldwork in Developing Countries*, edited by S. Devereux and J. Hoddinott. Colorado: Lynne Rienner Publishers Inc, 1993.

Hume, David. *A Treatise on Human Nature*, Oxford: Oxford University Press, 1739.

Ikelegbe, Augustine. "The Perverse Manifestation of Civil Society: Evidence from Nigeria," *Journal of Modern African Studies* 39(2001):1–24.

Kirk-Greene, Anthony H.M."*Conflict and Crisis in Nigeria*," Volume I and II, Oxford: Oxford University Press, 1971.

Kiss, Elizabeth. "Moral Ambition Within and Beyond Political Constraints: Reflections on Restorative Justice," in *Truth V. Justice*, edited by P. Rotberg and D. Thompson. Princeton: Princeton University Press, 2000.

Kritz, Neil. "Accountability for International Crime and Serious Violations of Fundamental Human Rights: Coming to Terms with Atrocities: A Review of Accountability Mechanisms for Mass Violations of Human Rights," *59 Law and Contemporary Problems* 127(1997).

Landsman, Stephen. "Accountability for International Crime and Serious Violations of Fundamental Human Rights: Alternative Responses to Serious Human Rights Abuses: Of Prosecution and Truth Commissions," *59 Law and Contemporary Problems* 81(1996).

Lee, Desmond. (trans.) *The Republic*, Plato, 2nd edition, Harmondsworth: Penguin, 1987.

Lett, James. "Emics and Etics: Notes on the Epistemology of Anthropology," in *Emics and Etics: The Insider/Outsider Debate*, edited by Headland Thomas, Pike Kenneth, and Harris Marvin. Newbury Park: Sage Publications, 1990.

Llewellyn, Jennifer J. and Howse, Robert. *Restorative Justice: A Conceptual Framework*, Prepared for the Law Commission of Canada, 1999.

Lockwood, Matthew. "Facts or Fiction? Fieldwork Relationships and the Nature of Data," in *Fieldwork in Developing Countries*, edited by S. Devereux and J. Hoddinott. Colorado: Lynne Rienner Publishers Inc, 1993.

Madiebo, Alexander A. *The Nigerian Revolution and the Biafran War*, Enugu, Nigeria: Fourth Dimension Publishers, 1980.

Mamdani, Mahmood. ""Truth according to the TRC," in *The Politics of Memory: Truth, Healing, and Social Justice*, edited by Amadiume Ifi and An-Na'im Abdullahi. London and New York: Zed Books, 2000.

May, Tim. *Social Research: Issues, Methods and Process*, 2nd edition, Buckingham and Philadelphia: Open University Press, 1997.

Mendez, Juan E. "Latin American Experiences of Accountability," in *The Politics of Memory: Truth, Healing, and Social Justice*, edited by Amadiume Ifi and An-Na'im Abdullahi. London and New York: Zed Books, 2000.

Meredith, Martin. *Coming to Terms, South Africa's Search for Truth*, New York: Public Affairs, 1999.

Mertus, Julie. "Truth in a Box: The Limits of Justice through Judicial Mechanisms," in *The Politics of Memory: Truth, Healing, and Social Justice*, edited by Amadiume Ifi, and An-Na'im Abdullahi. London and New York: Zed Books, 2000.

Moyle, B. *The Institutes of Justinian,* trans. 3rd Oxford: Oxford University Press, 1986.

Mulhall, Stephen and Swift Adam. "Liberals & Communitarians," 2nd Edition, Oxford: Blackwell Publishers, 1992.

Mustapha, Raufu A. *Ethnicity and the Politics of Democratization in Nigeria: Structure, Transformations and Processes.* Paper for Workshop on Ethnicity and Democracy in Africa, Queen's University, Kingston, Ontario, Canada, March 2000.

Nino, Carlos. "The Duty to Punish Past Abuses put into Context: The Case for Argentina," *100 Yale Law Journal 2619*(1991).

Norval, Aletta. "Truth and Reconciliation: The Birth of the Present and the Reworking of History," *Journal of Southern African Studies* 25(1999): 499–519.

Nozick, Robert. *Anarchy, State and Utopia*, Oxford: Blackwells, 1974.

Nwogu, Nneoma V. *Ethnic Revivalism: Recasting the Legacy of the Nigerian Civil War,* BA Thesis in Africana Studies, Wellesley College, 2002.

Oakley, Ann. *Experiments in Knowing: Gender and Method in Social Sciences*, Cambridge: Polity Press, 2000.

Obasanjo, Olusegun. *My Command,* Nigeria: Heinemann Ltd., 1980.

Oliver, Paul. *The Student's Guide to Research Ethics,* Maidenhead and Philadelphia: Open University Press, 2003.

Post, Kenneth & Vickers, Michael. *Structure and Conflict in Nigeria 1960–1966*, London: Heinemann, 1973.

Pronyk, Jason. *'Negotiating the Past': An Examination of the Methods Chosen by Rwanda and South Africa for Dealing with Justice*, MPhil Thesis in Development Studies. International Development Center, Queen Elizabeth House, University of Oxford, 2000.

Rakate, Phenyo K. *Transitional Justice in South Africa and the Former Yugoslavia- A Critique*, University of Witwatersrand June 11–14, 1999 Conference: TRC Commissioning the Past, 1999.

Rasavi, S. "Fieldwork in a Familiar Setting: The Role of Politics at the National, Communal, and Household Levels," in *Fieldwork in Developing Countries*, edited by Devereux S., and Hoddinott J. Boulder, Colorado: Lynne Rienner Publishers Inc, 1993.

Rawls, John. "Justice as Fairness," *Philosophical Review* 67 no. 2 (1958).

———. *Theory of Justice,* Oxford: Oxford University Press, 1971.

———. *Political Liberalism,* New York: Columbia University Press, 1993.

Roht-Arriaza, Naomi. "The New Landscape of Transitional Justice," in *Transitional Justice in the Twenty-First Century, Beyond truth versus Justice,* edited by Roht-Arriaza, Naomi and Mariezcurrena, Javier, Cambridge: Cambridge University Press, 2006.

Rotberg, Robert. "Truth Commissions and the Provision of Truth, Justice, and Reconciliation," in *Truth V. Justice*, edited by Rotberg R. & Thompson D. New Jersey: Princeton University Press, 2000.

Rubin, Herbert and Rubin, Irene. *Qualitative Interviewing: The Art of Hearing Data,*Thousand Oaks, California: Sage Publications, 1995.

Sadurski, W. *Giving Desert its Due: Social Justice and Legal Theory,* Dordrecht: Reidel, 1985.

Sarsby, Jacquie. "Special Problems of Fieldwork in Familiar settings," in *Ethnographic Research: A Guide to General Conduct,* edited by Rotberg R. & Thompson D. London: Academic Press Ltd., 1984

Schatzman, L. and Strauss, A. *Field Research: Strategies for a Natural Sociology,* New Jersey: Prentice Hall, 1973.

Scheman, Naomi. Unavoidability of Gender, in *Women, Knowledge and Reality. Explorations of Feminist Philosophy,* edited by Pearsall Marilyn, and Garry Ann. London: Unwin Hyman, 1989.

Shabas, William. The Sierra Leone Truth and Reconciliation Commission,' in *Transitional Justice in the Twenty-First Century, Beyond truth versus Justice,* edited by Roht-Arriaza, Naomi and Mariezcurrena, Javier. Cambridge: Cambridge University Press, 2006.

Shea, Dorothy. *Are TCs Just a Fad? Indicators and Implications for South Africa,* University of Witwatersrand June 11-14, 1999 Conference: TRC Commissioning the Past.

Snyder, Jack and Vinjamuri, Leslie. Trials and Error, Principles and Pragmatism in Strategies of International Justice, *International Security,* 28, no.3(2003): 6.

Soyinka, Wole. *The Open Sore of a Continent: A Personal Narrative of the Nigerian Crisis,* Oxford: Oxford University Press, 1996.

——. "Memory, Truth and Healing" in *The Politics of Memory: Truth, Healing and Social Justice.* edited by Amadiume Ifi and Abdullahi An-Na'im. London and New York: Zed Books, 2000

Sriram, Chandra Lekha. *Confronting Past Human Rights Violations, Justice vs Peace in Times of Transition,* New York: Frank Cass, 2004

Stanley, Elizabeth. "Evaluating the Truth and Reconciliation Commission," *Journal of Modern African Studies* 39(2001):525–546.

Stanley, Liz and Wise, Sue. "Breaking Out Again: Feminist Ontology and Epistemology," 2nd Edition, London: Routledge, 1993.

Suberu, Rotimi. *Federalism and Ethnic Conflict in Nigeria.* Washington, DC: Institute of Peace Press, 2001.

Teitel, Ruti. *Transitional Justice,* New York: Oxford University Press, 2000.

Tosh, John. *The Pursuit of History: Aims Methods and New Directions in the Study of Modern History,*" Revised 3rd Edition, London: Longman, 2002.

Tutu, Desmond Mpilo. *No Future Without Forgiveness,* New York: Doubleday, 1999.

Ukiwo, Ukoha (2003) 'Politics, Ethno-religious Conflicts, and Democratic Consolidation in Nigeria,' *Journal of Modern African Studies* 41:115–138.

Valdez, Patricia. "The Right to Truth," in *After the TRC: Reflections on Truth and Reconciliation in South Africa,* edited by James, Wilmot and Van De Vijver, Linda. Cape Town: David Phillips Publishers, 2000.

van Zyl, Paul. "Justice without Punishment: Guaranteeing Human Rights in Transitional Societies," in *Looking Back Reaching Forward: Reflections on the Truth and*

Reconciliation Commissions of South Africa, edited by Villa-Vicencio Charles, and Verwoerd Wilhelm. Cape Town: University of Cape Town Press, 2000.

Villa-Vicencio, Charles. "Getting on With Life: A Move Towards Reconciliation," in *Looking Back Reaching Forward: Reflections on the Truth and Reconciliation Commissions of South Africa,* edited by Villa-Vicencio Charles, and Verwoerd Wilhelm. Cape Town: University of Cape Town Press, 2002.

Villa-Vicencio, Charles and Verwoerd, Wilhelm. "Introduction," in *Looking Back Reaching Forward: Reflections on the Truth and Reconciliation Commissions of South Africa,* edited by Villa-Vicencio Charles, and Verwoerd Wilhelm. Cape Town: University of Cape Town Press, 2000.

Walzer, Michael. *Spheres of Justice*, Oxford: Martin Robertson, 1983.

Weber, Max. *Politics as a Vocation,* Muenchen, 1921.

Weschler, Lawrence. *A Miracle, A Universe: Settling Accounts with Torturers*, New York: Pantheon, 1990.

Williams. Anne. *Rhetoric as Cultural Performance,* Unpublished paper, BSA Medical Sociology Group Conference, 1983.

Wilson, Ken. "Thinking about the Ethics of Fieldwork," in *Fieldwork in Developing Countries*, edited by Devereux S., and Hoddinott J.Colorado: Lynne, 1993.

Zalaquett, Jose. "Balancing Ethical Imperatives and Political Constraints: The Dilemma of New Democracies Confronting Past Human Rights Violations," *43 Hastings Law Journal* 1425, 1992.

Newspaper Articles and Internet Resources

Brahm, Eric. "Truth Commissions," in *Beyond Intractability*, June 2004 <http://www.beyondintratability.org/essay/truth_commissions/> accessed January 29, 2007.

BBC News. "Liberia Sets up Truth Commission," International edition, February 21, 2006.

Daily Trust. *Oputa is not Welcome Here*, Paper Copy March 13, 2001.

Gamji News 1359 *A Sober Reflection on the Oputa Commission*, http://www.gamji.com/NEWS1359.htm, accessed Dec 18, 2003.

Gamji News 1399 *Oputa's Scale of Justice,* http://www.gamji.com/NEWS1399.htm, accessed January 3, 2004.

Gamji News 1444 *Reverse-Engineering a History of Institutionalized Ad-Hocism, Selective Amnesia, Executive Impunity & Group Euthanasia* http://www.gamji.com/NEWS1444.htm, (accessed January 3, 2004).

Guardian. *The Cleric as an Activist: Interview with Father Matthew Hassan Kukah,'* Paper Copy, September 7, 2003.

Human Rights Watch Nigeria: The Bakassi Boys: The Legitimization of Torture and Murder, *Human Rights Watch* 14, no. 5(A) (May 2002)[online]: <http://hrw.org/reports/2002/nigeria2/index.htm#TopOfPage> (accessed February 27, 2007).

Omoruiyi, Omo. *Refocusing the Oputa Commission (2) the Military,* http://www.nigerdeltacongress.com/rarticles/refocusing_the_oputa_commission%202.htm, (accessed Dec 18, 2003).

ThisDayonline, January 19, 2002, *Ethnic Groupings as Curse*, http://www.thisdayonline.com/archive/2002/01/19/20020119dis01.html, (accessed January 3, 2004).

ThisDayonline, July 9, 2002 *Dele Giwa: Between Law and Politics*, http://www.thisdayonline.com/archive/2002/07/09/20020709law09.html, (accessed January 3, 2004.

Today January 2–8, 2000.

Today January 9–15, 2000.

USafricaonline. *In The House of Mandela: A Silly Cry for Reparations,* by Nwankwo, Chimalum, http://www.usafricaonline.com/chimalum.mandela.html, (accessed January 3, 2004).

Valji, Nahla. South Africa: No Justice Without Reparation, *Open Democracy*, http://www.opendemocracy.net/debates/article.jsp?id=5&debateId=130&articleId=1326> (accessed Jan 21, 2007).

Vanguard. July 7, 2001 *How far can it go,* http://www.vanguardngr.com/news/articles/2001/July/07072001/f4070701.htm, (accessed January 3, 2004).

Vanguard, *Aisha Babangida's Wedding,* Paper Copy. July 10, 2003.

Vanguard, Paper Copy. February 13, 2004.

West Africa, Paper Copy. December 13–19, 1999.

Documents from the Human Rights Violations Investigation Commission

Instrument constituting a Judicial Commission of Inquiry for the Investigations of Human Rights Violations: Commencement: June 7, 1999 by Olusegun Obasanjo, GCFR, President, Commander-in-Chief of the Armed Forces of the Federal Republic of Nigeria. Federal Republic of Nigeria Official Gazette: Lagos, August 6, 1999. Volume 86 No. 56

Instrument constituting a Judicial Commission of Inquiry for the Investigations of Human Rights Violations: Commencement: October 4, 1999 by Olusegun Obasanjo, GCFR, President, Commander-in-Chief of the Armed Forces of the Federal Republic of Nigeria. Federal Republic of Nigeria Official Gazette.

Human Rights Violations Investigation Commission Sittings at the Women Development Center, Abuja, *Verbatim Report*, July 26, 2001.

Petition 1648:

I. The Violations of Human and Civil Rights of Ndi Igbo in the Federation of Nigeria (1966-1999). A Call for Reparation and Appropriate Restitution. A petition to the Human Rights Violations Investigating Committee by Ohaneze Ndi Igbo (The Apex Organization of the Entire Igbo People of Nigeria) For and on Behalf of the Entire Ndi Igbo, October 1999.

II. The Violations of Human and Civil Rights of Ndi Igbo in Nigeria, 1966-1999. Summary of Petition. Uraih, Ifeanyi Dr., Testimony, April 26, 2001.

Petition Ext. 64-1648:

I. Re: Alleged Violations of Human and Civil Rights of Ndi Igbo in the Federation of Nigeria [1966-1999]

II. Response by the Arewa Consultative Forum to the Human Rights Violations Investigation Commission (Oputa Panel), June 2001.

III. Addendum to the Response of the Arewa Consultative Forum to the Petition of the Ohaneze Ndi Igbo to the Commission, July 2001
IV. Arewa Summary of Response of the Arewa Consultative Forum to Ohaneze Petition, September 6, 2001

Petition Ext. 156-1648:

I. Memorandum Submitted by South-South Peoples' Conference, A Non-Partisan Political Organization, On Behalf of the Chiefs and Peoples of South-South Geopolitical Zone to the Justice Chukwudifu Oputa-led Human Rights Violations Investigation Commission (HRVIC), October 8, 2001

Synoptic Overview of the HRVIC Report: Conclusions and Recommendations including Chairman's Foreword, May 2002.

Unpublished Writings of Members of the Human Rights Violation Investigation Commission

I. Kukah, Matthew '*The Human Rights Violations Investigation Commission and the Struggle for Human Rights in Nigeria,*' Lecture given at the International Development Center, Oxford University.
I. Oputa, Chukwudifu I '*Professionalism, Shintoism, Loyalty, Allegiance and Patriotism,*' Unpublished.
II. Oputa, Chukwudifu '*The Struggle for a United Nigeria,*' Unpublished.
III. Oputa, Chukwudifu '*On the Human Rights Violations Investigation Commission,*' Unpublished.
IV. Oputa, Chukwudifu '*Composite Ruling on the Refusal of some Ex-Presidents and other Top Government Functionaries to attend and Testify at the Proceedings of the Human Rights Violations Investigation Commission,*' Unpublished.
V. Oputa, Chukwudifu '*Revenge Restoration of Harmony: Reconciliation and the Different Faces of Justice,*' Unpublished.

Interviews

Chief Dappa-Biriye, Chairman of the South-South People's Conference, Thursday, September 11, 2003. Port Harcourt, Nigeria.

General IBM Haruna (rtd), Member of the Arewa Consultative Forum and Signatory and Chief Witness to the Arewa Petition, Friday, September 19, 2003. Abuja, Nigeria.

Father Matthew Kukah, Member of the Human Rights Violations Investigation Commission, Friday, August 15, 2003. Massachusetts, U.S.A.

Chief Mogbo, Lead Counsel for Ohaneze Ndi Igbo, Monday, September 15, 2003. Enugu, Nigeria.

Barrister Nduka-Eze, Counsel for the Asaba People (Included in the Ohaneze petition), Thursday, September 25, 2003. Lagos, Nigeria.

Justice Chukwudifu Oputa, Chairman of the Human Rights Violations Investigation Commission, Friday, September 12, 2003. Oguta, Nigeria.

Chief Eze-Ozogbu, Chairman of Ohaneze Ndi Igbo, Tuesday, September 9, 2003. Enugu, Nigeria.

Mr. Uju Shariff, Media Consultant to the Human Rights Violations Investigation Commission, Saturday, September 20, 2003. Abuja, Nigeria.

Mrs. Chinwe Uwandu, Lead Counsel for the Human Rights Violations Investigation Commission, Tuesday, August 26, 2003. Connecticut, U.S.A.

Index

www.ingramcontent.com/pod-product-compliance
Ingram Content Group UK Ltd.
Pitfield, Milton Keynes, MK11 3LW, UK
UKHW012042150926
475560UK00001B/144

9 780739 122495